Compassion Conquers All

Teachings on the Eight Verses of Mind Transformation

By Tsem Rinpoche

NEW PAGE BOOKS
A division of The Career Press, Inc.
Pompton Plains, NJ

COMPASSION CONQUERS ALL
Cover design by Jeff Piasky
Printed in the U.S.A.

To order this title, please call toll-free 1-800-CAREER-1 (NJ and Canada: 201-848-0310) to order using VISA or MasterCard, or for further information on books from Career Press.

The Career Press, Inc.
220 West Parkway, Unit 12
Pompton Plains, NJ 07444
www.careerpress.com
www.newpagebooks.com

Library of Congress Cataloging-in-Publication Data

Tsem Tulku, Rinpoche, 1965- author.
   Compassion conquers all : teachings on the eight verses of mind transformation / by Tsem Rinpoche.
      pages cm
   Includes index.
   ISBN 978-1-60163-354-5 -- ISBN 978-1-60163-406-1 (ebook)
      1.Spiritual life--Buddhism. I. Title.

BQ5660.T72 2014
294.3'444--dc23

2014036131

Contents

དཔར་ཙེ་བླ་བྲང་།
SHARTSE LADRANG

Abbot Geshe Dakpa Tenzin
Gaden Shartse Monastery
Post Tibetan Colony-581 411
Mundgod, (N.K.)
Karnataka State, INDIA Phone :
0091 838

སྙོན་སྐྱིང་།

༄༅།། སྐྱིང་རྗེ་ཞེས་པ་ཆོག་མཛེས་པ་ཚམ་མ་ཡིན་པར་གཞན་དོན་ཁྱད་པར་ཅན་ཞིག
ཡིན། དེར་བརྟེན། འདི་ག་དགའ་ལྡན་དུ་རང་ཉིད་ནས་གཞན་དོན་དུ་རང་གི་དགོ་བའི་བཤེས་
གཉེན་དང་གྲོགས་དགོ་འདུན་གྱི་སེམས་གཏོ་བོས་བྱས་སྨྲས་བོ་སེར་སྐྱ་མཆོག་དམན་རིས་སུམ་མཆེད་
པའི་དོན་དུ་ཐུས་པ་མེད་པའི་ལས་ཀ་བྱེད་ཀྱིའི་འགོ་བཙུགས་པ་ནས་བཟུང་། ཚེམས་རིན་པོ་
མཆོག་ལ་གཞན་ནས་གུས་མཐོང་དང་དགའ་མོས་ཞུས་ཡོད། ལོ་མང་རིང་ཉིན་ཏུ་ཉམས་ཞན་པའི་
གནས་སྟངས་ཀྱི་འོག་ཏུ་གནས་སྐྱར། རང་ལག་གིས་ངལ་རྩོལ་གྱི་ཐོག་ནས་ཨར་ལས་ཀྱི་
སར་ལས་རོགས་ཞེན་ཏེ་མཁན་རྒྱར་བྱམས་པ་ཡེ་ཤེས་མཆོག་ལ་གཟིམ་ཁང་གསར་བསྐྱར་དང་།
གནས་འབོད་ཀྱི་སྲི་ཞུ་ལོ་མང་གི་ཁབས་འདེགས་བཏགས་བསྐྱབས་ཡོད། ལོ་ནས་ལོ་མཐུད་དེ་
ཁོང་ནས་དགོ་འདུན་གྱི་འཚོ་བའི་དོན་དུ་འདི་གའི་ཕུག་ཁང་ལ་རོགས་རམ་འབོད་བསྐྱལ་གྱི་ཡིག་གི
བྱིས་པ་སོགས་མཐུན་འགྱུར་རོག་རམ་གང་ཡིན་གནང་ཡོད། ཉེ་བའི་ཆར་རིན་པོ་ཆེ་མཆོག་ནས་
འདི་ག་གྲྭ་ཚང་དུ་ཚོས་རྣའི་རོ་ལེབ་སོགས་གསར་འདེགས་དང་། འདུས་ཚོགས་རིན་པོ་ཆེར་ན་བཟབ།
དང་རྟེན་སྐུ་བརྟན་བཅས་གུས་འཐུལ་མཛད་ཡོད། དེང་ཆར་རིན་པོ་ཆེ་མཆོག

Abbot Geshe Dakpa Tenzin
Gaden Shartse Monastery
Post Tibetan Colony-581 411
Mundgod, (N.K.)
Karnataka State, INDIA Phone :
0091 838

དཔལ་ལྡན་བླ་བྲང་།

SHARTSE LADRANG

ནས་འཕགས་ཚོགས་ཀྱི་འདུས་སྡེ་རིན་པོ་ཆེར་སྐྱབས་ཀྱི་རྩ་གནས་འབྱུར་ཏུ་རྒྱུའི་དགོངས་འཁར་མངོན་
བཞིན་པ་ཡིན། འདི་ག་གདན་ས་འི་སྐབན་ཕོག་དུག་བཅུ་བའི་སྐུ་སྐྱེར་རོས་འཛིན་ཕྱུང་བའི་
ལར་ཊ་བཞིན་དུ་གྲུ་ཆང་རིན་པོ་ཆེའི་ཐད་ལ་འདི་ལྟ་བུའི་ཐྲོ་སེམས་ཤེ་བ་དང་གདན་མའི་ཐད་ལ་
ཐུག་མེད་དཀའ་འལ་མཛད་པ་རང་ཅས་སུ་མངའ་བཞང་གནད་དོན་འདི་ལས་ལལ་ཆེར་ཤེས་སུབ་
པར་སྲུང་། དེན་གྱང་ནེ་འབོར་དུ་འབོད་པའི་གྱོང་གསེལ་ཁག་ལའང་། གྱི་དགོས་མེད་པའི་ཁིང་
གི་དགོངས་པ་བཞེས་ཚུལ་ལ་བརྟེན་ནས་ཙ་མཐམ་ཕན་ཕོགས་བྱུང་ཡོད། རྒྱུན་དུ་ངེས་མེད་དུ་
འཕེལ་བ་བྱུང་བའི་སྐྱེ་པོ་མང་པོ་དང་། ཕྱི་རྒྱལ་སྐྱོབ་ཕུའི་ཚོགས་མ་ང་པོ་ལའང་དེ་བཞིན་དུ་རོགས་
ཕན་བྱུང་དང་འབྱུང་བཞིན་པ་ཡིན། རང་དོན་ཡིད་བྱེད་ཀྱིས་མ་བཅིངས་པར་གཞན་གྱི་དོན་དུ་
འཚོ་ཞིང་གཞེས་པའི་ཚུལ་འདི་ལུ་བུའི་རྒྱལ་སྲས་བྱང་ཆུབ་སེམས་དཔའི་དང་ཆུལ་རྣམ་པར་སྲུང་
ཞིང་། རྒྱལ་འདི་ཉིད་ཚེས་རྒྱུད་བཟང་པོ་འདིས་གང་མཆོན་པར་བྱེད་པའི་དོན་གནད་དེ་ཡིན།

རང་གིས་ཉམས་སུ་ལེན་པའི་ཚུལ་འདི་ཉིད་ཚོམས་རིན་པོ་ཆེའི་དཔེ་དཔག་གསར་པའི་བཟོད་
བུ་ཡིན་པས་འདི་ནས་སྙོ་བ་ཆེན་པོས་གྲོག་བསྐུལ་བྱེད་ཚོག་པ་ཞིག་ཡིན། དགེ་བཤེས་གྱང་བང་
པའི་གསུང་རྡོ་སྐྱོང་ཚོག་བརྒྱ་མའི་ཕོག་ལ་རིན་པོ་ཆེ་མཆོག་ནས་གསུང་ཚོག་གནང་ལ་རྩམས་དེ་བ་
འདིའི་བརྟོད་དོན་དུ་འགྱོད་ཡོད། གསུང་འདིའི་ནང་དུ་སྙིང་རྗེ་རང་རྒྱུད་ལ་བསྐྱེད་ཚུལ་ནས་མཐར་
ཕུག་གི་ཡེ་ཤེས་མཚན་དུ་བྱེད་ཀྱི་བར་གྱི་ལམ་ལ་སྦྱོང་ཚུལ་གྱི་རིམ་པ་སྟེ། སྙིང་རྗེའི་སྤྲོར་ལ་བདག

Abbot Geshe Dakpa Tenzin
Gaden Shartse Monastery
Post Tibetan Colony-581 411
Mundgod, (N.K.)
Karnataka State, INDIA Phone :
0091 838

ཅག་གི་སྟོན་པའི་གསུང་གི་ཉིང་ཁུ་གྱུང་དྲུང་རིའི་གསུང་རབ་འདྲེས་སྐྱོན་ཞིང་འཛིན་འཛིན་འབས་ལ་ཡོད་འཁྲུལ་

བའི་ཆོག་བཅད་བརྒྱུད་ཀྱི་ནང་དུ་བདོག་སློབ་ནས་ཡོད་པས། ཆོག་གི་མཛེས་ཆ་དང་གི་དོན་གྱི་

ནུས་པ་འདིའི་ནང་དུ་དངས་ཆོས་གནས་པའི་ནུས་ལེན་གྱི་དོ་སྟོད་དང་། སངས་རྒྱས་ཀྱི་གོ་འཕང་

གི་གསང་བའི་གནད་བཅས་སྐྱད་ཡོད། ཆོས་ཆུལ་ཐབ་མོ་འདི་ས་སྟེང་རྗེ་ཉིད་ལ་འགྲོ་ཞིང་སྐྱང་རྗེ་

ཉིད་དོན་སྐུན་གྱི་ཕོག་མ་དང་བར་དང་ཐ་མ་སྟེ་སྐྱིང་པོར་ཉིད་པའི་མི་ཆོ་ཞིག་སྟོན་ཀྱི་ཡོད་ཅིང་།

ཆུལ་འདི་ཉིད་ཙེམ་པ་པོས་མཆོན་པའི་སྐྱལ་པའི་སྒྲུ་རྣམས་ཀྱི་རྣམ་ཐར་ཀྱི་ནང་དུ་དངོས་སུ་མཔོང་རྒྱུ་

ཡོད་པ་ཞིག་ཡིན།

ཆུལ་འདི་དག་ལ་བརྟེན་ནས། དཔེ་དེབ་འདི་འཆང་ཞིང་ཀློག་པའི་གང་ཟག་ཀུན་ཀྱང་

གཏན་གྱི་བདེ་བ་ལ་རེག་ཅིང་གཤུག་པའི་གཤིས་སུ་ཡོད་པའི་ཐེག་པ་ཆེན་པོའི་རིགས་སད་དེ་ཐར་

པའི་ལམ་སྲ་སྲིན་པར་གྱུར་ཅིག དཔལ་ལྡན་ཐར་རྗེ་བོས་བསམ་ནོར་གྱིང་གྲུ་ཆང་གི་མཁན་པོ་

ཀླུ་རམས་པ་གྲགས་པ་བསྟན་འཛིན་གྱིས། སྤྱི་ལོ་ ༢༠༠༦ ཟླ་༡༡ ཆེས་ ༤ དགེ་བར།

FOREWORD

BY HIS EMINENCE KENSUR RINPOCHE, ABBOT EMERITUS OF GADEN SHARTSE MONASTERY

Here we have a Teacher with a remarkable ability to, having absorbed the traditional Tibetan Buddhists teachings thoroughly, present them in a way that speaks directly to the hearts of people across cultures, backgrounds, cities, and religions. Tsem Rinpoche shows us in a profound, powerful yet accessible, humorous, and even playful way that compassion and loving kindness are a most natural part of us. For a modern audience, this is just what is needed to enlighten the mind. His own personal dedication toward putting compassion into action, through his continued works with monastic communities and individuals around the world, lends much weight to the qualities he always teaches and encourages in his own students.

The book contains Tsem Rinpoche's teachings on the Eight Verses of Thought Transformation. They are the heart essence of Lord Buddha's teachings on compassion, condensed into eight beautifully moving verses that cover the path from developing compassion to ultimate wisdom. From their simplicity unfold profound methods and qualities; within their beauty lies the true meaning of spiritual practice and the secret of Enlightenment. These teachings lead us to a way of life that revolves entirely about compassion—in the beginning, the middle, and the end; this is most perfectly reflected in the deeply compassionate living examples of tulkus such as Tsem Rinpoche.

May everyone reading this book find lasting happiness, awakening their innate, everlasting, compassionate nature—the very key to liberation itself.

HAPPY SUFFERING

A PRAYER FOR TRAVELERS IN THIS WORLD
BY H.E. TSEM RINPOCHE

Wherever I go or don't go—
everything I do can become Dharma,
because I do it
with a Dharma motivation.

Dharma motivation
arises from compassion.

Compassion arises from seeing
so many beings suffer
so much—
not knowing why,
not knowing what to do.

To liberate
the precious beings in the hells
created by hatred, suffering unbearable pain
I go on this journey.

To liberate
the precious hungry ghosts,
suffering the bottomless hunger and thirst of miserliness,
I go on this journey

To liberate
the precious animals
suffering helplessly and speechlessly
I go on this journey.

To liberate
the precious human beings
suffering from endless unfulfilled desire,
bleeding on the battlefields of birth and death,
soon reaping the bitter harvest of greed and anger,
I go on this journey.

To liberate the demi-gods
raging with the suffering of jealousy
and the long-life gods
blinded with the suffering of pride
I go on this journey.

For all who cannot join me
I go on this journey.

For those who have never
even heard the word Dharma
I go on this journey, because I care,
and cannot bear to see their pain
any longer.

To connect them with
the Buddha, Dharma and Sangha,
I rejoice in any difficulties and problems, and
absorb them for the benefit of all.

Not what I want, I will do, but what they need.

I pray to my most holy Guru
who is One with my Yidam and Protector,
who took this journey before, alone
and with so much more hardship than me.

"Please send me hunger and thirst,
pain and exhaustion,
sickness and poverty,
abuse and loneliness,

and

may I purify the hurts and harms
and difficulties of all mother beings and myself
by absorbing and enduring them happily."

In this way suffering becomes joy,
and every part of the journey—

happiness.

INTRODUCTION

EVEN A SIMPLE PRAYER...

DHARMA

Dharma teaches us the ultimate method, the ultimate way of release from samsara. When you receive the Dharma teachings—when you receive the method and you *practice* it—you will be able to free yourself from sufferings.

Just like a small seed planted in the ground can grow into a very large and very wonderful tree providing fruit for many, many beings for a long time, even a simple prayer invoking the blessings of the Three Jewels can bring tremendous results.

May all the great teachers and Masters
of all the religious traditions in the world—
Islam, Christianity, Hinduism, Judaism, Buddhism, all—
all the great Masters and their disciples have long life,
excellent health and happiness.
May their houses of prayer and their good teachings
grow and be able to benefit others.

We also dedicate that
His Holiness the 14th Dalai Lama of Tibet
and all the great Masters of the four lineages
and their students have long life, health and excellence.
May their precious enlightened prayers
come to fruition.

THE TEACHING

The teaching that I have the honor to give all of you—and I rejoice that you are able to receive—is called the *Eight Verses of Mind Transformation*, the *Eight Verses of Thought Transformation*, the *Eight Verses of Mind Change*, whatever you like to call it because there is no standard English translation. But it is eight verses or eight methods that we should follow as guidelines in our life to transform our mind, to become a person that is highly good for society and for the world.

Before we actually learn about the *Eight Verses of Mind Transformation*, I would like to talk a little bit about motivation, in dependence on the eight worldly concerns. That is very, very important—the eight worldly concerns and how they would affect my motivation, how the motivation will affect the action and its result.

RECEPTIVITY

It is the tradition of all Dharma talks, before the Dharma talk starts, that the teacher and the ones being taught should have a superior motivation. The one that is teaching should have received the transmission of the teachings and the lineage, should have studied thoroughly what has been taught and practiced it. I do not fit that qualification, but I will act like I do, so you play along with the act. We should have the transmission and we should be practicing it, and the motivation for teaching is to give you knowledge and the methods to become a fully enlightened Being. That is from the side of the teacher.

From the side of the student, one should be free from the three faults as explained in the *Lamrim*, symbolized by the three cups: the first cup having holes, the second cup having dirt and defilements inside, the third cup being turned upside down.

Dharma is very holy; it is very, very important. It is not entertainment; it is not something to be done when we are happy; it is not to be done when we have time; it is not to be done only when we are in a good mood. Dharma is something to be practiced 24 hours a day, constantly, vigilantly. Then you will get results.

So we should be free of the first fault, which is a cup having holes, which is not retaining, contemplating, thinking about, practicing the Dharma through a period of time. If we practice the Dharma through a period of time, there will be results. Absolutely, there will be results. And there is living proof of many people who have results.

We should be free of the second fault, which is the cup that is contaminated. So that means that receiving the Dharma should be received with a completely positive and good motivation. And the motivation is, on the lowest scope, to be free from the three lower realms; on the medium scope, to be free from the lower realms *and* to have compassion for others; and on the highest scope, you wish to receive Dharma solely for the sake of others, that you may become a fully enlightened Buddha to benefit others. Although all of the three scopes make you qualified to receive the Dharma, we will naturally develop the highest scope; that will be the most beneficial. Any other motivation—"I will attend a Dharma class to receive methods to gain wealth, merits, so I can change my luck and become rich, meet a girlfriend"— would be like a cup with defilements. When you pour something good into it, it is still unusable.

The third one is the cup that is upside down. To sit in a Dharma talk without an open mind—with your ears closed, falling asleep, bored or not wanting to accept, and just sitting there like it's a social event, and then whatever's said is said, whatever's not said is not said—is like a cup upside down. Whatever you pour into the cup, naturally it cannot retain it.

So we should be free of the three faults as symbolized by the three cups. This is very important.

AUTHENTICITY

We cannot just listen to made-up Dharma talks. It will be of no benefit. So the authenticity of the teaching must be revealed, and then the person giving it to you must have the lineage himself or herself. Without that, you will not receive any transmission or blessings.

The original teachings on the *Eight Verses of Thought Transformation* originated from Buddha Shakyamuni himself. Buddha Shakyamuni initially developed Bodhicitta and acquired the merits of both profound insights and great deeds for three countless eons, finally achieving Great Awakening.

LINEAGE BLESSINGS

After Buddha Shakyamuni became enlightened, he gave the teachings on compassion to his disciples, which were then passed down to the great Indian Buddhist Panditas Arya Asanga and Nagarjuna, and from them to highly enlightened Beings such as the great Shantideva. Shantideva was the one that actually emphasized, reiterated, and expanded on the talks of compassion by the Buddha, and he put it into words that were easier for us to understand. The teachings on thought transformation arose from this text called *Bodhicharyavatara*, which is development of Bodhicitta, great compassion. Shantideva was the one that made the practice of Bodhicitta very, very famous.

After that, it came to the great Lama Serlingpa who was the root Guru of Atisha. Atisha came from India and later went to Tibet and spread the Dharma all over Tibet to countless disciples. The Mind Training teachings he passed down only to his main disciple, a layman who was one of the previous incarnations of His Holiness the 14th Dalai Lama, the great Je Dromtonpa.

Dromtonpa, in turn, practiced and achieved this teaching and passed it down chiefly to the monks Geshe Potawa, Geshe Sharawa, and Geshe Langri Tangpa.

GESHE LANGRI TANGPA

So Geshe Langri Tangpa received the teachings from Dromtonpa directly. He thought it was very profound and felt it would be a tremendous loss if they were not preserved. These teachings were profound, yet simple, and until then not practiced publicly, but only passed down to a few, very qualified disciples.

Before the great Geshe Langri Tangpa passed away, he wrote it down for the first time. Before Geshe Langri Tangpa, it was always given orally, never written down; there was no text. So Geshe Langri Tangpa, out of great compassion, decided that the teaching must not be lost and wrote it down.

Years later, after he had passed away, one great Master called Geshe Chekawa found a piece of scripture, one verse of a teaching that said, "May I accept unjust loss and offer the victory to others."

Geshe Chekawa was very intrigued, moved, and touched by this statement, because this statement represents the essence and the complete embodiment of all Buddha's teachings. This sentence contains all of Buddha's intent and all of Buddha's teachings in one line: "May I accept unjust loss and offer the victory to others."

Determined to meet the author of the text, Geshe Chekawa went all over looking for him. When he came to one of the students of Geshe Langri Tangpa, he found out that the Master had passed away. In a small town near Lhasa, he met another Master called Geshe Sharawa, who was practicing the Mind Training teachings. He received more and more teachings from him, and Geshe Chekawa started to teach it openly to others, openly in public teachings, like now.

From Geshe Chekawa, down a long line of teachers, these teachings were passed on until they reached the great King of Dharma—Je Tsongkhapa. From Lama Tsongkhapa to his disciples such as Khedrup Rinpoche and Gyaltsab Rinpoche, this was passed down a long line of Lamas, to His Holiness Pabongkha Rinpoche, to His Holinesses Trijang and Ling Rinpoche, and down to His Holiness the 14th Dalai Lama.

I received these teachings, the transmission, blessing, and commentary, in Washington, New Jersey in 1979. I was 13 years old at that time, but I remember it very clearly: His Holiness was sitting on a throne, in the mountains, there was a white butterfly circling him through the whole time, and there were rainbows in the sky for a week—I saw it myself—hovering over His Holiness giving this talk.

And that was the first time that I had the honor and great fortune to see His golden face, and this was the first teaching I ever received from His Holiness.

I was very moved, and I was in tears for many hours while His Holiness was teaching this. I was in tears because I knew what it contained was the truth. It moved me, it touched me, and I wanted to practice it—*practice* it. I don't know if I am actually practicing it well or not, but I made a strong determination and prayers in front of His Holiness at that time that I will be able to practice this. So today I pass the teaching down to all of you.

Although I am not qualified, His Holiness is qualified, so I invoke His blessings and I invoke His grace that all of you may be able to learn, understand, and practice these holy teachings.

PART ONE

RENUNCIATION:
GIVING UP SELFISH CONCERNS

MOTIVATION

THE EIGHT WORDLY CONCERNS

When we do any kind of Dharma activities—lighting incense, making prostrations, making offerings, offering flowers, giving donations to the temple, giving *dhana* to monks, sweeping the temple, driving or buying supplies for the temple, being committee members for the temple, meditation, chanting—anything—it should be free from the eight worldly concerns, or the eight worldly Dharmas. Dharma means conduct. So Buddhadharma is correct conduct, conduct that leads to awakening. The eight worldly concerns are:

> *to be happy when we are praised,*
> *to be unhappy when we are insulted,*
> *to be happy if we receive any gifts,*
> *to be unhappy if we don't,*
> *to be happy upon achieving reputation,*
> *to be unhappy when we are unsuccessful,*
> *to be happy when we are comfortable,*
> *to be unhappy when we are not.*

We should not be practicing the Dharma for these reasons at all.

It will be better to memorize those eight worldly concerns than 100 tantric practices, and I am not trying to blow your mind away. But yes, if you know the mantras and practices and all the initiations of 100 tantric deities, but you are practicing with the eight worldly concerns, you will not achieve even one tantric result of one tantric deity.

So we should memorize the eight worldly concerns and check over and over and over again if we are free from them. And if we are not, we must work on it immediately, we must get over it, we must practice, and we must immediately get to the point, because time is short and time is running out. So any Dharma actions should be free of those eight worldly concerns.

If our Dharma is preoccupied with them, there are many disadvantages. When we do actions with the eight worldly concerns, the act will lead to rebirth in the lower realms, and future lives will be also spent with uncontrolled attachments, like now.

All results of uncontrolled delusions, attachments, and negative states of mind *now* are a sign that they have not been controlled in the past. So if they were not controlled in the past, the result is that we have not gotten it under control at this time. If it is not gotten under control *at this time*, it can only get worse, not better. So future lives will also be spent with uncontrolled attachments. One cannot ever enter the Mahayana path. One cannot reach liberation.

If you do any Dharma actions with the eight worldly concerns—whatever practices that you do, you will not gain liberation. One will constantly experience hindrances in one's meditational practices: hindrances of laziness, sleepiness, procrastination, doubt, and instability. That is the inner level. The outer is financial problems, time constrictions, responsibilities, and so on.

So when we practice Dharma in a way that the motive is not free of the eight worldly concerns, then the results of course will not be positive; while we are practicing, we will experience many inner and outer obstacles, and there will be no fruition of our practice—except planting seeds for our future lives.

The practice then becomes only a service to the eight worldly concerns. What happens when you practice the Dharma with any of the eight worldly concerns is that it actually *feeds* the eight worldly concerns. How is that? You might practice the Dharma so that you will be praised. Yet the point of practicing the Dharma is not to be praised and not to be recognized. The point of practicing the Dharma is to reach liberation. So if you help a Dharma center or you meditate wonderfully when people are around, yet when no one is around, you pick your teeth, then you are not practicing the Dharma with a correct motive.

So when our friends are around, we raise our eyebrows, the whites of our eyes are there, we have great meditation experiences, we see lights, our hair goes up, and our tears come down. But if the minute our friends disappear, we go out for a coffee break, I think we are practicing Dharma for praise.

If you are practicing Dharma for praise, the very practice of Dharma leads to wanting more praise, increasing of the big ego, therefore leading you to the three lower realms. You may think, "Hey, how can practicing the Dharma lead us to the three lower realms?" Practicing the Dharma doesn't lead you to the three lower realms; your negative intent before the action leads you to the three lower realms.

You could sweep out an old folks home with a good motivation—"May this act benefit others"; that act will lead you to Buddhahood.

You can sit in front of Je Tsongkhapa and meditate for five hours, and meditate on the U.S. dollar and meditate so your finances move up and that you can get some wealth vase, some wealth mantras, some wealth pujas (and that you will pass on everything to make it on Sunday for the wealth prayers) then—if you meditate for five hours in front of Je Tsongkhapa, you are meditating for material gain.

Meditation doesn't mean fulfilment of your worldly wishes. Meditation and practice is for Enlightenment. Therefore when we do practice for the reason of getting praise, how can we label that Dharma practice? That is definitely not Dharma practice. In fact, that very motive makes the act result in the fruition of more negative karma. So when we start practicing Dharma, instead of our wish to get praise decreasing, it increases. The more we go to a Dharma talk, the more we know, the more empowerments, the more teachings, the more knowledgeable, the more scholarly we become, the more advanced we do it, the more we can chant, the more we can teach, then the bigger our ego, the bigger our pride, the bigger our arrogance. Everything becomes bigger. And the whole point of learning Dharma is to decrease those points and to, in fact, annihilate or destroy those points.

So when you practice Dharma with the wrong motive from the beginning, it is not the Dharma, the Dharma teacher, or the Dharma environment that is at fault. It could be your ignorance at fault, or it could be that you know it and you have not applied the antidotes hard enough. It is definitely not the Dharma.

I always use the example that if you do not know how to drive a car, and the car has a little accident, it is not the fault of the car but the driver. So if you do not get results from your Dharma practice, it is definitely not the Dharma. It is definitely not the Dharma teacher, it is definitely not the Dharma itself, it is not the center, and it is not the Dharma students. It is you yourself.

Because if Dharma had no results, our altars should be empty. There should be no enlightened Beings. So we would be prostrating to empty things! And there would be no living enlightened Masters today, such His Holiness the Dalai Lama, His Holiness the great Karmapa, His Holiness Sakya Trizin, His Holiness Dudjom Rinpoche, His Holiness Dilgo Khyentse Rinpoche, and His Holiness the great Gaden Tri Rinpoche. There would not be any enlightened Masters around, like my Master His Eminence the great Kensur Rinpoche—they would not be around.

But there *are* living beings around that are enlightened and highly realized and extremely beneficial for others: the great Chinese Mahayana Master, the nun Reverend Cheng Yen in Taiwan—definitely she's a Master of practice. She's doing a lot more than I can ever do. She must be advanced in her practice to be able to do that. So there *are* living examples around us of people who are practicing and practicing correctly.

Therefore, why we are not getting those results? We must point the finger back at ourselves. Not at the Buddhas, the Dharma, the temple—"Oh I couldn't listen, because it was so hot and I was sweating; it is not my fault"—or the Dharma teacher, or the Dharma texts, or the Sangha.

We must go back to the source. If the Dharma or the Dharma teacher or the Buddhas were at fault, as I said, the altars should be empty. But because there are living representations of the result of correct Dharma practice, the Dharma must be correct and we ourselves must be at fault. But we should not be despondent or depressed. If we are at fault, the fault is impermanent, dependent on conditions. Therefore we can change the conditions and bring an end to the wrong practice and start on the right practice.

So when we do Dharma practice to get praised or to avoid insults, that is a very low aim, and the minute we don't get praise we stop doing Dharma practice. So the fault is not Dharma—it's the motive.

If we do Dharma practice to get gifts, to avoid not getting gifts, to get ang pows (red-colored envelopes containing money, which are traditionally used in Chinese custom as gifts or presented to the Lamas or Sangha as a sign of respect) and all that, the minute we don't get it, we get upset. Again it is not the Dharma; it is our motive.

If we do Dharma for good reputation—"Oh, he's so good, he's so holy, he's such a good person, he's a family person, he also goes to the temple, and he's so wonderful"—the minute we stop getting praise, we suffer, we feel despondent, we don't want to meditate, we don't want to practice, we don't want to join the temple, we don't want to listen to the Dharma, we don't want to meditate, and we become despondent. Why do we become despondent? Not because we have not gotten the results, but the actual reason is the very motive that we started with—out of ignorance—was wrong. So the Dharma is not at fault.

Then, we wish to get Dharma to receive some material gains—success. So we go to the temple to listen, hoping it will change our luck. We go in front of the altar, kowtow to change our luck. We make offerings to change our luck, we listen to the Dharma and recite lots of mantras, we go to empowerments to receive great blessings to change our luck so that we can hit the lucky number, our economic situation moves up, and we can get rich.

I get a lot of this question from people: "I've been chanting and praying; why isn't my business moving up?" Because the very reason you are chanting and praying is not for your business to move up. So you should be chanting and praying regardless of whether your business moves up or not. Otherwise the minute your business doesn't move up economically, *you* go down. Of course it is a normal human reaction that you feel sad and unhappy, but that is when you should actually increase your Dharma practice and increase your Dharma energy. You should take advantage of the situation.

If we practice the Dharma to move our economic situation up—that our company moves up, we can make more money, our stocks go up, whatever—and if that doesn't happen, we become despondent. We have used the Dharma for a short-term benefit, and we don't derive the ultimate benefit from Dharma, which is complete freedom from suffering, not just business moving on.

When we practice Dharma, when we see Lamas, get divinations, get blessings, do rituals, and sponsor pujas for the sake of simply receiving wealth, increasing our wealth as an end in itself, then the Dharma has been brought down to a very low level, and the full purpose of Dharma is not fulfilled.

So we should not practice Dharma with the intent that it will move our economic situation up, or to avoid the economic situation from going down. If we do that, our rebirth will be in the spirit realm.

So whether you practice Dharma or not, if you are always miserly and selfish, always concerned about money—you would do anything for money—your rebirth will be the spirit realm anyway. But if you practice the Dharma, you have a chance to purify that karma, so it will be better to be a Dharma practitioner who is greedy and miserly and worldly about money than a non-Dharma one. Because whether you are a Dharma practitioner or not, you still have the same faults. So it would be better to have the faults *and* Dharma, and there is a chance that you may not take rebirth as a spirit, and if you do, the time is less; the duration of that rebirth is less.

Whether you practice the Dharma or you don't practice the Dharma, your problems are exactly the same. If you look deeply, whether you practice the Dharma or not, your situation, your problems arise from karma, not Dharma; they do not arise from your relationship with Dharma. So therefore, whether you practice the Dharma or not, you have the same problems. But with the Dharma, if practiced correctly, it becomes a temporary remedy to help you get over your problems and also gives you ultimate methods to get over your problems.

How much effort you put into the practice is how much result you will get. So we should practice the Dharma without any of these eight worldly concerns. It is very important.

Then we should not practice the Dharma simply when we are comfortable—when everything is going right, when everything is going comfortable, when money is okay, family is okay, when there is harmony; the minute one of these goes out of balance, we stop the practice. If we are going to stop the practice because of that, we might as well not even begin, because those things will happen anyway. Why? We are in samsara; we have been in samsara for hundreds and hundreds and thousands of lifetimes, and we have created the karmic causes and dispositions for disharmony, for financial problems, for difficulties to arise.

But it is out of fear, and knowing that those difficulties will arise, that we must look for a method. What more superior method than to destroy the roots of those karmas before they bear fruit, by Dharma practice? If we practice the Dharma sincerely, we will definitely get the results.

The first step is motivation, and our motivation should be based upon the guidelines of the eight worldly concerns. It should be free of those eight worldly concerns from the very start. But don't be even more despondent, thinking "Well, what about all the things that I've done? What about the *dhana* I have given? What about the pujas? What about the prayers, the meditations, the offerings on my altars?" There is benefit, but it would be even greater and more efficacious if it was done free of the eight worldly concerns.

Antidotes to free ourselves from the eight worldly concerns are basic guidelines for us to follow to reshape and recondition our conditioning. They are guidelines, not restrictions. Some of us think, "Oh, Dharma's so complicated. There are so many restrictions; there are so many minute details." Yes, there are, because *we* are complicated, *we* are full of minute details. So if the Dharma is an antidote to this, then the antidote will match the problem.

For example, when we go to school there are examinations, requirements, and points that we need. We need to get there on time, do our homework, and so on. It's years and years and years of restriction and requirements, and that is quite difficult. But when we finish school, the actual regimentation, requirements, and the regulations we followed lead to freedom. What freedom? When you get your degree, you can get whatever job you want, *you* pick what you want to do.

It's the same in Dharma. It is like school. When you follow the Dharma correctly, you follow its regulations and rules; this restraint leads to total freedom in the future. So we shouldn't think of Dharma as a prison wall; we should think of it as very kind guidelines given by an enlightened Being to help us follow our good path. And it will bring immediate results. It will bring immediate results, but the motive must be correct.

If one follows the eight worldly concerns, one is not better than an animal. Because an animal wishes to be praised, receive food, receive good reputation—the males fight with each other to get the best females. They wish to be very comfortable; they wish not to be unhappy. It's the same. What's the difference between us and the animals, except that we do things in a more sophisticated manner?

So we must think that if we practice Dharma or we live our lives with the eight worldly concerns, we are the same as animals, although we are not. And because we are higher and better than animals, we should have a motivation that is much better.

NOTHING NEW IN SAMSARA

The objects one sees are the projection of one's deluded mind. So everything that we perceive—this is good, this is bad, this is nice, this is not—is the result of our own negative karma. If the object we perceive is inherently existent in itself, is real in itself, then everybody who sees that object must see it the way we see it. Yet everyone that sees an object will see it differently because the result of their karma is different.

Change the object into one you are not attached to.

There is nothing new in samsara. Think. You hang around here—there is nothing new. All the food that you want to eat, you have eaten; all the clothes you like to wear, you have worn; you have driven all the cars. You have been everywhere, you have done everything. You have slept, you have eaten, you have taken all types of medications, you have gone to all types of entertainments, you have tried all kinds of things. There is nothing new in samsara. You have done this for lifetimes and lifetimes, and when you die, you will be doing it for more and more and more lifetimes.

There is nothing new in samsara. There is nothing exciting to hang around for; there is nothing exciting to be attached to. Everything is the same, so shouldn't we practice the Dharma, free of the eight worldly concerns, to become a Buddha to benefit others? Wouldn't that be a breath of fresh air?

If we do things on the basis of the eight worldly concerns, we will not have true happiness. In fact, we will have more suffering, whether we practice the Dharma or not. Sufferings come about by wrong actions; wrong actions come about by wrong motive. So whether you have the wrong motive and do wrong actions through the Dharma or not, it does not matter. *It does not matter.*

NO CHOICE: NOTHING LASTS

You must realize that everything is impermanent by nature. No choice: nothing lasts. What is the definition of impermanence? Any phenomenon—any item, object, thought, place, people, situation, whatever—that is dependent on other causes or phenomena for its existence, is impermanent.

So therefore, people who are attached to praise, and whose happiness arises from receiving praise, their happiness is deluded because praise is dependent on a lot of things. It is dependent on our actions, dependent on the stability of our actions, and then dependent on actually getting the praise and having the people around to praise you. And when you don't get it, you become unhappy. So praise is impermanent. It is not lasting. So if we depend on happiness from praise, we will experience unhappiness again and again and again and again.

It is the same if our happiness is dependent on wealth or achieving wealth, and only wanting wealth. Wealth and the process of achieving it takes up a lot of time, takes up our youth, takes away our time from our family, takes away time from everything; there are lots of sacrifices such as health and mental peace. We can even go off the deep end to achieve wealth—do negative actions, things that break the law.

And then when we actually achieve the wealth, the wealth is unstable; we can lose it anytime. Achieving it requires so many causes, and the causes themselves are impermanent. Therefore, if we base our happiness on wealth and achieving it, and the process of achieving it, we will suffer very badly.

PERVASIVE IGNORANCE

We will suffer constantly while we are trying to achieve it; when we achieve it, we will suffer, as there is no guarantee that we will be able to keep it. And the minute we lose it or there is a sign of losing it, we run to temples, we run to Lamas, we run to divinations, we run to magicians, we run to fortune tellers, we run to anybody who can save our wealth. And in the process, we suffer. Then when we actually lose it, we suffer even more—for some, extremely. From beginning to the middle to the end, it is total suffering—mental, physical, environmental, outer, inner—constantly.

And our ignorance is pervasive and very strong to say or think that if we achieve that, we have happiness. If we look around at people who are actually wealthy, how many of them are deeply at peace or have happiness in their minds? And when they have it, when they lose it, how do they feel? And that is the process of life. One day, you will lose it. If not in life, definitely at death. When you are born, you are born naked; you cannot take anything from your previous lives.

WRONG PERCEPTION

When we think about it carefully, when we think about it constructively and from the right angle, all phenomena are empty of inherent existence. Empty of inherent existence does not mean empty of existence; it means empty of the way we perceive it exists. Therefore, when we check something, when we look at something, when we have attachment toward something, it in itself does not exist the way we perceive. For example, wealth does not provide happiness, but we have a wrong perception that it does—we follow that; we run after that. And it is not that if we don't achieve wealth we become unhappy; it is the wrong perception to believe it brings happiness. And when it does not bring happiness, we suffer.

It is not the wealth or losing it that makes us suffer. It is a wrong perception—the ignorant perception of what we think it can do for us. So it is the motive and the process that make us suffer. It is our wrong perception or idealization that make us suffer. Not the wealth, not losing it, nor not achieving it.

WRONG PROJECTION

We can apply these examples with everything around us, in everything that has happened in our lives that has so-called "disappointed" us. It is our wrong projection and wrong attachment to it. It is not the object itself.

All objects are free of inherent existence. Inherent existence means existing on its own without causes. If wealth could exist on its own without any causes, it could bring us happiness because it would be permanent. So if something can exist *on its own*, without dependency on causes, it will be permanent. If these things are permanent, they will bring happiness. Because wealth comes under the classification of impermanent phenomena, our grasping at it as being permanent when it is not makes us suffer.

It is like when we meet someone new; if we have a projection that this person is kind, compassionate, honest, and will be loyal, and we find out later they are not, it is not that which makes us suffer. It is our wrong projection of that person, what we think they should be like, but they didn't fit our projection. It is because of our wrong projection of that person, or that phenomenon, that we suffer—we do not suffer because of that person or that phenomenon.

So we go on ignorantly blaming other people, other situations, other things. And from that wrong projection and wrong perception, we shout, we scream, we hurt, we use harsh words, we kill, we steal, we lie, we commit sexual misconduct, we use schismatic speech, we put others down. It is from that wrong perception we do all those negative types of actions. Those negative types of actions will bear fruit. Because the root is negative, of course, the sprout—what the result will be—is negative.

WHAT MAKES US SUFFER

So what makes us suffer is not realizing that things do not inherently exist on their own. Every phenomenon is impermanent. It is our stubbornness not to accept that fact and to put more into it than it is; it is our stubbornness to have the wrong projection toward an object of the five senses and it not fitting our projections, the way we think it should be, that makes us suffer.

And the worst part of it is that we do not have enough wisdom, clarity of mind, meditational powers, and penetrative wisdom to actually see an object for what it really is. Therefore we are stuck with two problems: first, wrong perception due to delusional mind, due to wrong mind and wrong perception, and second, a grasping at the wrong projected perception. So grasping at the wrong projection and wrong projection itself makes us suffer.

GRASPING

What is grasping? I will give you an example, the same one I gave previously: when we meet someone and feel that they should be a certain way, and we build up our hopes, that is grasping—onto the way we think they should be. And when that person does not fulfil what we thought they should be through *our* lack of wisdom, then we think, "*They* are bad, *they* are evil, *they* are negative, *they* are not good; *I* must fight them, *I* must get revenge, *I* must get them back."

So it is actually not them, if we use our wisdom. *It is not them.* It is our wrong perception and our lack of wisdom to perceive. The lack of wisdom to perceive and the wrong perception itself are *also* impermanent, which means it can be removed, because these two factors are based on other conditions to survive.

Therefore there *is* an end to suffering.

Logically, because those very perceptions are impermanent, that is a clear implication that there can be eradication or annihilation or destruction of those actual causes that bring us unhappiness. Think about it. All our sufferings arise from wrong perception of or wrong projections onto everything around us.

From morning to night, we have wrong projection. That wrong projection can come from conditioning; it can come from stubbornness, laziness, and selfish attitude. Ego is what makes us basically have wrong projection. And then having that wrong projection and acting out on that wrong projection brings unhappiness. Please think about it. This point is extremely crucial. We should pray to Manjushri and Je Tsongkhapa for this realization, not for anything else.

Check everything in your life—everyday for 24 hours, from the time we were born until now—the acts we have done are based on our projections. Some of them wrong, some of them correct. Now, think carefully.

The minute we stop this, or train ourselves in stopping this, the sufferings start to lessen. The problem may remain the same, but you suffer less, and that is the point. And when you suffer less, you have clarity of mind and therefore the ability to solve it. That is the whole point.

When you practice Dharma and you have a wrong projected expectation that your problems will be solved immediately, *now*, that is very demanding of the Buddhas. (And it's not that the Buddhas are not going to acquiesce or agree to your demands.)

All of the problems and difficulties arise from that. And the more we add on to projections, the more we reinforce it and condition it. We condition it and we condition it again and again and again, and our sufferings increase, increase, and increase. Even if we get wealth, even if we get cars, money, houses, fame, our sufferings become even more intense to the point of suicide, to the point of going crazy. That is why people who have many things suffer greatly, and people who don't have anything suffer greatly. Either way, you suffer because the cause of the suffering is within you. Think about it! So how can you go to the Buddhas, go to Jesus Christ, go to God and pray constantly that your sufferings cease when you do not lift one finger to actually remove the cause of suffering?

When you realize that point, and start acting in ways that start cutting out conditioning, wrong view, and wrong projection, you will see your sufferings lessen, even if you have many problems to endure. And that is how great Masters, great Dharma practitioners, are always happy, always willing, always enthusiastic, always ever-ready to help others, even though they may have hundreds of people criticizing them, hating them. They endure many difficulties, many problems—financial, physical, health, environmental, social. They may go through many different types of sufferings and problems, yet they will go on, teach, practice, help, and never lose their enthusiastic perseverance because they have realized that point. That is the reason, because they have realized that point.

Until you realize that point, you are in samsara—your own samsara. Samsara is not a wheel on the wall in which you get reborn, from this realm to that realm; we all have our own samsara. And that is the crucial realization we need to have in order to cut it. Samsara is another word for suffering. Think about it!

So to support that growth, that meditation, that realization, or that understanding, we must continuously collect merits. So when we start to change our luck, *that* is the luck we should change. That is why we make offerings to the Three Jewels, serve our Gurus, study the Dharma, meditate, chant, recite mantras, go on retreats and pilgrimages, offer incense, offer joss sticks, serve the Sangha, do charity works, and so on. That is the reason to collect merits: to be able to support the growth of those realizations. When you can support the growth of those realizations, your sufferings lessen and eventually stop. That is why the purification of negative karma and the collection of positive karma is so crucial and important in our practice.

We may think that making offerings on an altar, cleaning, doing our prayers, is so menial and so small and it is not real Dharma practice. Wrong view! Anything done in relation to the enlightened Beings creates extremely powerful propensity. How much we put into it is how much we will get back. Buddha Shakyamuni has said he was asked by one of his disciples, "When the Buddha is alive and when the Buddha is present, making offerings to the Three Jewels in the form of Buddha Shakyamuni allows us to collect a great amount of merit and to destroy vast amounts of negative karma. When the Buddha is not physically here anymore, what shall we do?"

Then the Buddha replied, "When I am not around, making offerings to an image in the likeness of myself and believing it is me will be equal to making offerings to me in person and directly."

So when we uphold the images of Buddhas and put beautiful ornaments and gold, and make beautiful offerings and make a place for them, and make an effort for them, it is the same as having the actual living Buddhas themselves in your presence. And any actions that you do within their presence is the same as the amount of merit you would collect if you actually did it for them in person. And that is a direct quote from Buddha Shakyamuni himself, not from one of his disciples, an Indian pandit, or a Tibetan Guru.

So we should be ever-persevering in making offerings, maintaining our altar, making prostrations, making mandalas, Vajrasattva, doing our meditational deity practice, studying up on the Dharma, meditating and—most important—applying it in our daily lives. In fact, we should be ever-persevering, because that will become the root cause for cutting out suffering. We should contemplate this.

We should not be like the cup with holes: we hear it, say it is correct, pray, go home, then go back to the same thing day after day, month after month, year after year, with no improvements and some danger of degeneration. We should be like a cup without holes, and retain it, think about it, contemplate it, study it, and especially collect merits to support it. If we don't, we can be in Dharma for 10 years, 15 years,

20 years, but will never change, never transform. In fact, the ego becomes bigger: "I am a *senior* Dharma practitioner. You should listen to me. I've met 20 Rinpoches. I've done 50 rainy season retreats."

Wonderful! But you are still going to hell—you are still suffering. Wonderful, but let me see the results. The result should be obvious—a changing and transformation of your character. So let's not leave the Dharma talk despondent. We should leave the Dharma talk happy that we have some kind of realization and try to make a change in our lives and transform. Now, this moment, today, from today on. And maintain it by study, practice, and the relationship with our Gurus, if we have one. We should maintain it.

FROM EFFORT TO EFFORTLESSNESS

And by that constant nurturing, like a small child, it will grow into adulthood, able to protect and watch itself, able to take care of itself. Like that, these realizations will come to the point where they are irreversible, where without effort they remain steady and constant: effortless giving, effortless patience, effortless enthusiasm, effortless compassion, effortless Bodhicitta—it will become effortless.

DHARMA IS A MIRROR

On that basis, every phenomenon is empty of true existence. Free of inherent existence—not existing on its own right. It is existing on causes. Because it is existing on causes, once we cut the causes, it cannot exist anymore. In the case of delusions—negative mind—we can stop it.

It would be very good if we can memorize the eight worldly concerns. Commit them to memory and make sure that we can recite them every day. People like to recite a lot of mantras; people like to recite a lot of long sadhanas and intricate, complicated deities with a lot of hands, a lot of arms, a lot of legs, a lot of consorts. How many legs, how many arms, how many consorts, what's their color, what are they carrying in their hands? We like to have those pictures and have those statues and go to those initiations and show them to our friends and tell them how holy, intricate, and complicated, and how high we are with these high initiations. But in the end when we check, the very fact that we like to show off to our friends shows that the motive is incorrect.

I am not here to criticize you, and I am not here to tell you that all of you do have these worldly motivations, that you are all so naughty. In order for you to not have those types of motives, you must understand them, the faults behind them, recognize them, and that can only come from hearing about them. We should not think that the Dharma is insulting us; we should think that Dharma is a mirror for us to reflect our actions within. So whatever we do, we reflect it in the mirror of Dharma to see if we are doing it correctly or not.

The Dharma should be treated like a mirror; the Dharma teacher should be the mirror-holder; and the Sangha should be the ones polishing the mirror. And we are the ones looking into the mirror. So, it's very important that we see the

Dharma as a mirror for us to reflect our actions. And when we do any type of action, we should immediately check it with the Dharma to see if it is correct or not. If it is not, we should not feel insulted, we should not feel despondent, and we should not feel that "I can't do it." In fact, we should be very happy that there is something we can check it with to improve.

We have a guideline out of samsara. By renouncing samsara, worldliness, self-centeredness, we become real people. We become human beings—beings with compassion.

PART TWO

COMPASSION:
IT IS IN OUR HANDS

THE EIGHT VERSES OF
MIND TRANSFORMATION

Check ourselves out! How many years have we been doing Dharma? How many Gurus have we chased? How many Rinpoches, how many divinations, how many things have we done? Why are we not transforming? Because the very motive might have been wrong, and along with that, we have wrong projection and a lack of merits. It is very clear, very concise, and very logical.

So therefore, in the beginning, correct motivation is very important; in the middle, correct motivation is very important; and in the end, correct motivation is very important. When motivation is correct, there will be wonderful, positive, lasting results. There is definitely an end. On that logical basis, I have just established with your intelligent and educated minds the fact that suffering can come to an end.

Do you want it to come to an end? It is in your hands.

We should have the motive to practice the Dharma, to go to the temple, see our Gurus enthusiastically, with perseverance, with great patience, with great love, with great understanding of the great value that will arise from there, by being free from the eight worldly concerns, the eight wrong motives—which is a guideline for developing our motivation. And the wrong motivation is also impermanent; it is dependent on causes. The cause is ignorance. Once you have been given wisdom and knowledge, ignorance is cut. When ignorance is cut, the very foundation for wrong motive is cut. So, what's left? Positive motive.

Therefore, we should not have the motivation to do any action—especially Dharma action—to get praise, to avoid insult, to receive gifts, to be unhappy if we don't, to avoid bad reputation, to try to get good reputation, to try to receive comfort, and try to avoid discomfort. It should be free of this.

The motive should be Enlightenment, freedom of suffering for everyone.

I will get into developing that compassion, step by step by step. We all want compassion; we like getting compassion; we like having compassion; we like being around compassion. So why don't we just *be* compassionate?

Now we will talk about how to develop it.

Please let Geshe Langri Tangpa's holy words sink in slowly:

By realizing that all sentient beings
Are more precious than wish-granting jewels,
For attainment of the supreme goal,
May I always hold them dear to my heart!

Whenever I associate with anyone,
May I view myself as least of all,
And, from the depths of my heart,
May I cherish others as supreme!

During all actions, as soon as thoughts
Or delusions arise in my mind
That are harmful to myself and others,
May I stop them with effective means!

As for sentient beings who are bad-natured,
When I see they are oppressed by negativity and pain,
May I cherish them just like I am encountering
A precious treasure that is difficult to find!

May I accept unjust loss
Such as others abusing me,
Or slandering me out of jealousy,
And may I offer the victory to others!

And if someone I have helped,
One for whom I had great hopes,
Harms me without slightest reason,
May I view him as my holy Guru!

In brief, directly and indirectly,
I offer aid and joy to all my mothers!
May I secretly take upon myself
All harm and suffering of my mothers!

May all of this be undefiled
By stains of the eight mundane views,
And through discernment, knowing all things as illusion,
Without grasping, may all be released from bondage!

VERSE ONE

ALL BEINGS ARE PRECIOUS

By realizing that all sentient beings
Are more precious than wish-granting jewels,
For attainment of the supreme goal,
May I always hold them dear to my heart!

It is said that if we wash a wish-granting jewel three times, polish it three times, hang it on top of a huge banner and ask for anything, it can provide all of our basic food, water, and necessities.

Yet sentient beings are far more precious, because their existence enables us to achieve the state of great awakening. No such claim can be made of a wish-granting jewel. The key point is that if there were no sentient beings, there would be no individual awakening. Without sentient beings, we cannot practice compassion. Without compassion, we cannot attain Bodhicitta. Without Bodhicitta, we cannot become an enlightened Being.

Therefore, the kindness of sentient beings and the kindness of Buddhas are equal.

Sentient beings are even more precious than a wish-granting jewel. All sentient beings, everyone around you—enemies, friends, neutral people—are very important to you because it is in dependence on them you achieve Enlightenment. How is that? How do you practice patience if you have no enemies to develop patience with?

And what Buddhas are there without patience? What Buddhas exist with no patience? We need to have patience, and the only way we can develop it is by someone helping us, and that someone is an enemy.

So an enemy is just as precious as someone that benefits us, because without them, *how do we practice patience?* One of the definitions of a Buddha is that he has patience. If we become a Buddha with no patience, if we hate enemies and we are a "Buddha," I don't think we will end up on the altar! So think!

We need to practice generosity. Who do we give things to? The trees? Waterfalls? Mountains? "I offer this gold to you, mountain...." No, it is to sentient beings. They are very kind to allow us to help them, that we are able to practice the *paramita* of *dhana*—giving. If we want to go one step higher, to our Dharma brothers and sisters—giving, helping the Dharma institutions, the Sangha, and if possible, if we have one, to our root Guru. It is their kindness that allows us to practice the *paramita* of giving.

Every Buddha has tremendous spiritual and unlimited, inexhaustible wealth, and where did that come from? *Giving.* Giving to sentient beings. So in order to develop wealth, in order to develop karma to even be rich in your next life, you are dependent on others. So when you are so dependent on others, how can we not respect others? They give us an opportunity to give, as well as to practice enthusiasm, perseverance, and so on.

We want to become a Buddha, so we must love every single sentient being that exists in the six realms. Let's say, there are five billion sentient beings in this world, and we love 4,999,999,999, but we don't love one for any reason, guess what? You cannot become a Buddha. How can a Buddha love everyone except *her*? Except *him*? "I love everyone! I love every single sentient being except that one!" Think about it!

Your actual Enlightenment is dependent on every single sentient being, and your attitude and motive toward them. So they are very kind to exist to let you develop this. If we show a bad face, a sour face, if we engage in bad talk, gossip, negativity, if we shout and scream and hurt and abuse others, we don't realize how precious they are. They are just as precious as the Buddhas; they are equally precious, according to the *Bodhicharyavatara* by Shantideva.

If they are equally important, do you think you can pray, kowtow, make offerings to the Buddha and the Three Jewels, your Guru and the Sangha, and turn around and abuse other sentient beings and become enlightened? You are in some weird cult, because that is not what the Buddha taught. We have all been guilty, including myself, of following this weird cult. In front of the Buddha, we kowtow, we prostrate, we have tears. Then we turn around, someone bothers us, and we complain, "Hey!" We have done that over and over and over.

The Buddhas are important because we need their teachings, we need their blessings, we need their inspiration, we need their guidance. We need the Three Jewels. We need them 50 percent. And in order to fulfill what they have taught us, where is the object to act out what they have taught us? Sentient beings. That's right—*all* sentient beings. Neutral ones, hated ones, and loved ones. And the very fact that you have hated ones and neutral ones in your vocabulary shows that you are not practicing Dharma. Think. It is all so inter-connected and so logical.

So how can we just prostrate to the Buddhas, prostrate to the Sangha, prostrate to our Guru, to our altars and not show equal reverent respect to everyone else? Of course you don't have to run around with lotus candles and light one for everyone you meet and say, "I respect you and pray to you." Of course you don't have to be that fanatical. The point here is to have a sincere respect for other sentient beings. That includes your wife who gets on your nerves, who nags; that includes your husband who gets on your nerves, who comes home from work at eleven o'clock; that includes your kids who shout and scream non-stop; that includes loving the Guru who shouts at you.

You've got to love everyone, everything. We should start with our Gurus, we should start with our wives, and we should start with our husbands. Have we been mistreating our wives? Have we been talking angrily to our maids? Have we been mistreating our husbands and talking wrongly to our husbands? To our friends? To our relatives? Have we? If we have, I don't think we are making progress here. And if we are not making progress, we are going to suffer.

Of course there are certain people who really get on our nerves. We don't have to beg, hug, and kiss them, and say, "I love you!" and hold their hands for 24 hours and say, "Look,

Guru! I am practicing compassion!" You don't have to do that. The point is, let them be the way they are, but don't hate them. You may avoid them for now, with the reason that you have not yet fully developed compassion. Until you have fully developed compassion, you don't want to have any hate. Or you want to protect yourself for now, but that cannot go on forever—"I hate them, I want to protect myself, so I stay away."

So we have got to love all sentient beings to become enlightened. If we don't, how do we become enlightened? Impossible! So to become enlightened, 50 percent is dependent on sentient beings. We should start today, now, this moment to start loving our wives, start loving our husbands, start loving our children, our relatives, our parents, our aunts and uncles, our Sangha members, our Gurus, people that are neutral to us, people who we just met, and especially enemies. We should start!

Stop kowtowing to the Buddhas, because that is just 50 percent of the game. If you kowtow to them, it means you will follow what they are saying. You respect what they are, what they represent, what they teach you, and therefore you kowtow. So if you kowtow and you turn around to do the opposite, you should get an Oscar award for your brilliant acting. And we all should get an Oscar because we are the greatest actors on Earth. All of us! Think about it. It sounds funny but it is true—that's why it's funny!

We have to respect everyone; we have to respect every-thing. And we must start with the people who are easiest for us to respect—from our Gurus to the Sangha, to our Dharma brothers and sisters, to other religious practitioners, to neutral people, to enemies. Without that deep respect, 50 percent of your practice is not there. A table cannot stand with two legs. Think about it. We need to start practicing this.

Please, practice that first verse. That verse has such deep meaning. Let's become real Dharma practitioners. We have received the first verse; let's put it into action, let's make it stable, and let's make it constant. And let's support it and make it constant and stable by offerings to the Three Jewels, prostrations, meditations on meditational deities, mantras, and so on.

I implore you, my old friends and my new friends, to please put this teaching into practice. This moment.

MEDITATION

What would it be like to perceive every living being as infinitely precious?

How would my body feel?

How would my emotions feel?

How would my heart and mind feel?

How would I interact with them?

Allow yourself to breathe in these liberating energies and relax within them. Let them become one with you.

VERSE TWO

SEE ALL BEINGS AS BUDDHA

Whenever I associate with anyone,
May I view myself as least of all,
And, from the depths of my heart,
May I cherish others as supreme!

If we practice these eight verses alone, we can gain Enlightenment. No joke. Without initiations, without altars, without deities, without anything—if we practice this, from our heart, our sufferings will stop.

If we have problems, we should apologize; if we have difficulties, we should make up. And we should see the root of the problem and stop it from our side.

Never mind whether the other person stops it or not. That is not your problem. When you die, you die alone. When you go, you go alone. When you make karma, you make karma alone.

Now you may say the purpose of Dharma is to become happy. Happiness here is not defined as happiness for the self alone, though. It is happiness for all sentient beings. So if we do Dharma for happiness for the self alone, then it disqualifies us as a Mahayana Dharma practitioner.

Mahayana or non-Mahayana, we cannot become a Buddha without the qualification of wishing sentient beings *metta* and love, and wishing them to be free from sufferings. One of the definitions of a Buddha is that he or she has that quality. Therefore, without that quality—whatever labels you like to put, Mahayana or non-Mahayana—we cannot achieve Buddhahood.

Dear friends, why run away, avoid, deny? Why not give in to concern and acting for others, acceptance, patience and calm abiding, because that's who we really are? If that's not so, why does Buddha teach us to find that within ourselves? If Enlightenment is not within, where might it be?

When we go deeper and not only hold others dear, but see them as supreme, it is their inherent Enlightenment that we focus on. When the prison bars of pride are broken, the flower of humility can blossom. Our view becomes pure.

Due to bad karma, we get wrong views. Due to wrong views, even our spiritual teachers or Buddhas that may appear to us will be perceived as impure. Guru devotion is the training to be able to humble ourselves, to put our ego, put our pride, put our knowledge, put everything down in front of our Guru whom we visualize as the Buddha. In learning to do that, we are able to apply it to everyone else. It starts from there.

Humility is the name of the game.

MEDITATION

What would it be like to perceive every living being as very exalted, worthy of my deepest reverence?

How would my body feel?

How would my emotions feel?

How would my heart and mind feel?

How would I interact with them?

Allow yourself to breathe in these liberating energies and relax within them. Let them become one with you.

VERSE THREE

SAMSARA IS A STATE OF MIND

During all actions, as soon as thoughts
Or delusions arise in my mind
That are harmful to myself and others,
May I stop them with effective means!

"Checking the mind" is to be aware of the ever-changing contents of the mind without being carried away by them; it is the foundation and essence of Dharma practice and something we can and should be doing at all times, whatever we do, wherever we are. If we take our thoughts, ideas, and emotions seriously and allow them to cloud our perception with wanting and not-wanting, they seduce us into many actions motivated by greed and anger, which always end in pain and disaster—not only for us, but for all those connected to us in any way, which, ultimately, is everybody and everything.

We should confront disturbing attitudes by realizing they are like clouds that appear and disappear without solid substance, and avert confusion and damage by focusing on the pure, unchanging awareness that is like the sky. Because most of us are not yet able to dissolve afflictive emotions directly in this way, we must apply their antidotes.

If everything that exists is impermanent phenomena, there must be an end. So my afflictive emotions which arise from the self-cherishing mind are impermanent phenomena. Why? In order for my self-cherishing mind and ego to exist, it must have causes and conditions. So if the causes and conditions are removed, the ego or the self-cherishing mind can be removed.

Now, what we need to do is to find out what are the causes and conditions for that ego to exist and to apply the antidote. It's very simple. We have all been told it can be removed. We have all been told that our mind is clarity, luminous nature, and clear light, and we have been told over and over by great Lamas like His Holiness. But when we leave the teachings we are wondering, "Okay, I am clear light. Why I am not clear? Why I am still getting angry?"

What are some of the causes? Not understanding the truth, not understanding the Dharma, not having wisdom, not having a collection of merits. Reconditioning yourself in it. Not trying to root it out or pull it out. Not dealing with it or facing it directly. So our negative states of mind are dependent on a lot of causes. When we start removing the causes, that negative state of mind must disappear. Therefore, there is an end to afflictive emotions, to negative states of mind which bring about negative actions of body, speech, and mind that bring about negative results.

These negative results that we experience individually are samsara. Samsara is not a place we go to. It is an experience that we have, an experience we all have. Why? If samsara is a place we go to, everybody in this place must suffer. His Holiness is in this so-called samsara and he doesn't suffer, but we are here and we suffer. Therefore samsara cannot be a place, it must be a state of mind that is brought about by our personal, individual fruition of karma. Very simple.

Think carefully, if I cannot benefit others, at least I should not be a trouble-maker. Don't gossip, don't incite problems, don't incite skepticism, don't talk about people behind their back—don't ever talk or make comments about other people. If they really are what you are commenting about, people will know eventually, whether you "helped them along" or not. So whether or not you gossip about people, people will know what that person is like. People are not stupid; people can see. So it's better never to gossip and talk about people behind their backs.

So if we cannot benefit others, at least we won't make trouble. Don't be a trouble-maker. And if a trouble-maker comes around, don't make trouble for them. I think that is very important. That is the essence of the teachings and everything that we teach leads to that.

Develop penetrating insight into that point. How do we develop penetrating insight? By contemplating on a point again and again and again, and if it benefits, to think about these benefits again and again and again. To contemplate it, put it into your mind and recondition it slowly. Definitely—I promise—your afflictive emotions endangering others and yourself will become less. No doubt. There are many examples of people like that.

MEDITATION

What would it be like to be fully aware of but detached from the contents of my mind, and when unhappy impulses arise to dis-identify with them (be free of them), instead of compulsively acting them out (be enslaved to them)?

How would my body feel?

How would my emotions feel?

How would my heart and mind feel?

How would I interact with them?

Allow yourself to breathe in these liberating energies and relax within them. Let them become one with you.

VERSE FOUR

A GOLDEN OPPORTUNITY

As for sentient beings who are bad-natured,
When I see they are oppressed by negativity and pain,
May I cherish them just like I am encountering
A precious treasure that is difficult to find!

Beings of negative dispositions, with sufferings, may I cherish them as if I have found a precious treasure. What!? People who make me suffer, people who are with afflictive emotions, who are ugly and negative and mean—to hold them dear and precious? What!? Where is that crazy monk going now? Now he is going to brainwash me into loving my enemies!

No, I am not going to brainwash you. I am going to give you the reasoning behind it. That statement shocked everyone, no? And some of us have a lot of enemies, so we need this. We need to hear and practice it. When we practice it, the enemies—from our point of view—disappear. We become happy.

Think, "When I see beings of negative disposition and suffering, may I cherish them as if I have found a precious treasure which is difficult to find." Incredible! When I come across beings that are oppressed by violent sufferings and overwhelmed by their delusions, and are bad-tempered and bad-natured, may I cherish them as if I found a precious treasure. Why? Because they are more precious than a wish-granting jewel. Why is that? A wish-granting jewel can confer on you some material gains, but a negative person or a person who hurts you can confer on you *Enlightenment!*

How is that? Because they give you the greatest opportunity to practice patience, compassion, and love. They are the greatest test to see if you have compassion and love, and if years of meditation and practice have brought any results.

Because if you see them and still feel like you'd rather not see them, what are you chanting for? Why are you praying and who are you kowtowing to? Who are you praying to? You must be praying to a weird demon on your altar; you must be praying and prostrating to your ego.

So this is the meter in which to check: if something around you disturbs you. If someone is doing something that disturbs you, it's not them. The fact that it disturbs you shows you that *you* are disturbed. We look at it from a positive and broader perspective and angle. When people do things around you that disturb you tremendously and you can't help but to make it known and react, it shows that you are disturbed and that your self-cherishing mind is so strong and so powerful and so pervasive in your body that you must let the other person know it bothers you. (So don't do it!)

You might say, "I have a good motivation." Forget it. The very fact that it disturbs you tells you that you are disturbed! Disturbed by what? By your afflictive emotions that are so strong and your selfish mind that is so strong. And your self-grasping mind—that mind that says, *I* am important, *me, myself, my* happiness, *my* wishes, *my* concerns, *my* comfort is more important than you. So I will tell you, "Your dress is ugly. You shouldn't wear that. The way you talk disturbs me. You shouldn't be doing things like that." And so on. In fact, 99 percent of the criticisms—nice or not nice, gentle or not gentle—that we direct at others, all come from the self-cherishing mind.

The great Atisha, who was such an enlightened Being, had one monk in Nalanda who hated him. He was an older monk who only saw bad points in Atisha and who criticized him. When Atisha gave teachings, he would never attend. He would influence others and say, "Don't go to the teachings." He only criticized Atisha over and over and over, and tried to make his life difficult in the monastery.

If it were me, I would have dropped an H-bomb on that monk immediately, but because Atisha practiced these teachings, you know what he did? When the great goddess Tara told Atisha to go to Tibet to teach the Dharma, Atisha invited this monk with him to go to Tibet and he sponsored his whole trip. And you know why? No, not because Atisha was a fruitcake. It was because he wanted to practice patience and love. And this was the best person to practice through, because Atisha didn't have anyone who didn't love him; he only had people who praised him. There was only one person who hated him, who constantly criticized him and constantly wanted to debase him.

So Atisha said, "Hey, what a golden opportunity! Come along with me to Tibet." He was there for 13 years with this monk who criticized Atisha to his dying day. And Atisha said wonderful prayers and held a ceremony and funeral for this monk to get a good rebirth.

Atisha's practice is as famous as Buddha Shakyamuni's in Tibet. In fact, we have lineages and teachings today because of Atisha. Even the Tara practice which exists today is because of Atisha. Offerings—Atisha taught us how to make offerings to collect merit. Wealth vases—all of us run to different Dharma centers to get wealth vases; the first person to teach us how to make wealth vases and to contain the energy to get wealth was Atisha. He was the one who wrote the original *Lamrim*. He was the one who disseminated the monk vows which spread all over Mongolia and Tibet. Because he was a pure monk, he inspired many others to become monks.

This great Lama served and compassionately took care of the old crony of a monk who had nothing but the ugliest things to say about him. Imagine that! We are not willing to do that, or we think that Atisha was crazy for doing that. But when we look deeper, Atisha saw a golden opportunity to practice patience, love, and compassion, because there was no one that hated him. He found one person and said, "Oh, it's my opportunity. I want to make sure that I destroy the last traces of my negative emotions so I can become a Buddha to benefit others." That was his motive.

When I meet others who are oppressed by violent and intense pain, and are overwhelmed by their negative emotion, may I cherish them as if I found a precious jewel, a precious treasure. *That's* why: because they *are* a precious treasure. They offer you the opportunity to develop the points that you need to become a Buddha.

Therefore when you go to a Dharma center, when you meet funny salespeople, funny waiters, funny relatives, funny friends, and funny Dharma brothers and sisters, jump on them, hug them, love them, kiss them, and give them gifts and prostrate to them if you want to be a Buddha! You may think it is ridiculous, and I am not saying actually physically do that, but do it from your mind! What an opportunity to practice the Dharma! Jump on them! Hold their hands and don't let them go. If they think you are crazy, who cares! You'll be a Buddha! That is what Je Tsongkhapa did. That's what Atisha did. Think about it.

So the next time you meet someone mean and rude, and who only abuses you, you should have a little smirk and say, "Hmmm... how lucky I am! What a golden opportunity!" Seriously, you should immediately pray in your heart and say, "I will practice these teachings, and I will treat this person well." Of course, we cannot treat our enemies and people that hurt us well overnight, but let's not keep using that excuse for not practicing.

I ask you to please read over the stanzas everyday as a daily practice. Incorporate it into your meditations and re-contemplate on it. These practices are core. If you practice this alone and nothing else, you can gain Enlightenment. This is the most profound, the essence, the heart of Buddha's teachings. Out of deep respect, because these are so important and so meaningful for everyone, I implore you and ask all of you to please read over them every day and with time, you will internalize them and when a certain situation arises, that corresponding verse will come into your minds. Guaranteed. And then you will be able to practice and advance and advance and advance.

MEDITATION

What would it be like to feel gratefulness instead of fear or anger in very difficult relationships, because here I can learn to become independent of others' attitudes toward me? To accept them as they are, and to love them as they are?

How would my body feel?

How would my emotions feel?

How would my heart and mind feel?

How would I interact with them?

Allow yourself to breathe in these liberating energies and relax within them. Let them become one with you.

VERSE FIVE

ACCEPTING DEFEAT, YOU WIN

This body is not me; I am not caught in this body.

I am life without boundaries.
I have never been born; I will never die.
Look at me, look at the stars and the moon —

all of them are me, manifestations of me.

Thich Nhat Hanh

May I accept unjust loss
Such as others abusing me,
Or slandering me out of jealousy,
And may I offer the victory to others!

This verse is the very foundation of Bodhisattva practice. The reason we take Bodhisattva vows is to have guidelines and to promise to follow those guidelines to become a Bodhisattva—to become enlightened. So if we practice this verse and understand its significance and meaning, then the foundation is provided.

If we are able to offer the gains and victory to others, even in daily life, we will benefit tremendously, purifying so much karma and generating so much merit. Whatever the outcome in worldly terms, gain or loss, all will be like a great victory to us. Compassion conquers all.

Don't be attached to external results; every saint has started small. Some of them were much worse than us. For example, Milarepa was a magician who brought murder, black magic, and hailstorms on his enemies. But he became enlightened. We hung out at Hard Rock Café, and we are not enlightened. He definitely did worse than we did, but he is enlightened. Please remember this.

This is the hardest practice. We will always have people jealous of us. We will never be free of it. You need to accept that fact. Why? Because many beings are stuck in samsara. They are stuck in their delusions. They are ignorant of the delusions. They are ignorant of what jealousy can do to them, the harm it can afflict on them and others. And as a result of thousands and thousands and thousands of life-times of conditioning, they act out of jealousy. So what makes you think you have the power for them not to get jealous of you and abuse you and slander you? Some of them even have the audacity and the great "courage" to slander Buddhas, Bodhisattvas, their Gurus. So what makes you an exception? What makes me an exception?

You are going to be the object of other people's jealousy if you are doing well—not necessarily that you are at fault, but because their delusions are out of control and they have no wisdom to control their delusions. They act out of delusions, and the delusions that they act on bring negative states of existence for them again and again and again.

By reacting to these people negatively, you increase your delusions and you increase theirs. So when someone treats you badly and you treat them badly back, you are just as bad as they are. Your delusions are just as strong as theirs. Your ego and self-cherishing mind are just as strong as theirs. You are not better. Yes, they may have done something to you, and it is wrong and they are wrong. But when you react similarly, you are equally wrong. So when someone treats you badly or says something bad to you, hurts your feelings or is rude to you, and you are rude back and you are short-tempered back, you are just as bad as they are. You are just as guilty. Two wrongs do not make a right. You should be just as ashamed as they are! And you, in fact, collect the same amount of negative karma that they do—the same. If they treat you badly and you treat them badly back, what is the difference? Who cares about the cause anymore?

The action creates negative results. The very fact that you treat them badly and you abuse them shows how uncontrolled you are and how much you are without compassion. You do not consider how they might be suffering. You do not consider their situations. You are not sensitive to them and their sufferings. And your not being sensitive to them shows how strong your self-cherishing mind is; you are more important than them, so you do not need to be sensitive to them.

In fact, when someone treats you badly, abuses you, or is rude to you, this is the moment for you to check if you are doing Dharma practice. And if you are not, that is the moment to start. If you complain, if you make noise, if you make a big issue of it, if you run around like a chicken with no head, screaming and shouting, you look just as bad.

If someone mistreats you and is rude to you, or does not talk nicely to you, or is not being kind to you, as a person trying to practice the Dharma, you have found a perfect opportunity. What do you think? When everything is good, and everyone is polite and nice, that's when you recite mantras and you sit there with your eyes rolling and incense blowing, chanting, "Ommm"? No!

When do you practice Dharma? When you are *not* chanting, when you are *not* praying, when you are *not* in retreat, when you are *not* near your Guru, that is when you practice the Dharma. When someone shouts at you, when someone scolds you, is rude to you, has abused you, is hurting you; doesn't agree with you, or opposes you, that's when you practice the Dharma.

May I accept the unjust loss and offer the victory to others. Why? In that acceptance of defeat, *you win.* Because it shows your negative mind is becoming less. So when someone reacts negatively to you and you react negatively, you are just as guilty; you look just as ridiculous. And you should be just as embarrassed.

In fact, you should react in a way that says, "What is bothering you? What happened?" Explore. Check. Have compassion and see if maybe they are having a bad day, or if they are not having a bad day, maybe they are oppressed by violent pain, overwhelmed by sufferings and delusions. Isn't that an object for you to treasure, to cherish, and to practice with? Because without that, how do you practice patience?

If we do not offer the victory to people who treat us with abuse and slander and so on, we are going to be fighting one battle after another after another. And we will never, ever win the battle because there are going to be many people who would treat you in that way; they have treated you in that way, they are treating you in that way, and they will continue to treat you in that way. And whether you practice the Dharma or not, they will still treat you in that way. So what is the best remedy? Fight back or practice the Dharma?

What is the benefit here? What's the gain? If you practice the Dharma, you will be able to deal with these types of people, and as a result, you will start improving. You will start changing; you will start becoming a better person. And therefore, you win the ultimate war, not the little battles. And after a while, when you practice enough, even when people are rude and mean to you, you can still treat them with compassion; you know that you are improving in your practice. You know you are going in the right direction and you should be proud without ego; you should be happy, rejoice, and dedicate the merits so that you can increase that positive emotion even more.

May I accept unjust loss, such as others abusing me, or slandering my out of jealousy, and may I offer the victory to others. When we listen to it, it is beautiful, we praise it, we touch it to our head, we make offerings, and we kowtow to it. We kowtow to the people who practice that teaching. We respect the people who talk about that. We respect it, we kowtow to it, we make offerings to it, we make an effort to go listen and learn about it. Why? Because deep down inside, we are good human beings; we would like to practice that, and we know it's the truth. Deep down inside, we know it is correct, it is the truth. Therefore we admire it and praise it, and we would like to practice it.

The next step is to *actually* practice it. The next time when you meet someone who is delusional, angry, and hateful, who doesn't want to co-operate, who is difficult, think about the story I told you about Atisha and the monk who scolded him constantly. We should always think about Atisha and that mean, old monk. Every time we want to react, we should think of Atisha. If we can't remember, we should wear a pendant of Atisha, and when that emotion arises—flash it! We should get statues of Atisha, make pictures of Atisha, and put them in our cars, on our dresser tables, in the living room, in the office. Especially in traffic, we should have pictures of Atisha to remind us how he treated that monk who abused him so much and how we should practice. Atisha treated that monk so well that he became enlightened.

Another thing is, any abuse, any unhappiness, and any suffering that you get from others is an effect resulting from a cause; without a cause, there is no effect. So ultimately, you yourself, myself, ourselves, all of us have created the cause. We have done things in our previous lives and in this life to get that effect, to receive that effect. So it's better to receive it with patience and humility, *offer the victory to others, suffer the loss,* purify that karma, train our minds and advance. Wouldn't that be more beautiful?

These beautiful words, aren't they music to the ears? Every single being on that altar that we bow to embodies that message. We make offerings to them because they embody that quality. So being that we respect the qualities that these holy Beings embody so much, doesn't it behove us to try to achieve it?

And how do we achieve it? One step at a time—one jealous, abusive, negative, hurtful person at a time. And in fact, if you really want to practice the Dharma, you should set up a little stall that says "Abuse me, slander me, show me disrespect, hurt me, do something to me, please. I want to become a Buddha. Please! I want to be a Bodhisattva. Please, please, please, PLEASE!"

And when someone does, we should sit there with a big smile—happy, excited—and say, "Can you come back tomorrow and do it again? Can we make an appointment?" Most of us, when we see them coming, we get in a bullet train and scram! But in fact, every person that abuses us—this is not a psychological mind game—is the result of our negative karma on one hand and an opportunity to practice on the other. And when they do that to us and we can't offer them victory, it is a meter to see how much we have practiced or not practiced. So in fact, these beings should be held as rare ones and precious treasures. Why precious treasure? Because these beings can confer the six *paramitas*—giving, patience, ethics, enthusiasm, meditative concentration, and wisdom—onto us. They allow us that opportunity. They allow us the opportunity to practice, and without them, we cannot become enlightened, as I explained to you all, my friends. It is dependent on all sentient beings that we can gain attainments.

So as I have told you, if there are five billion people on this planet, and you love 4,999,999,999 and there is one being that really gets on your nerves and you hate him, guess what? You can't become enlightened. You can't become a Buddha. You can't even get the higher results. You can't get even an ounce of Bodhicitta. Forget ultimate Bodhicitta, not even relative Bodhicitta. Because your Enlightenment depends on them. You need an object to have compassion for. You need an object to be compassionate to, to offer the victory to, so that you can become a Bodhisattva. Your level of Bodhisattvahood depends on them, depends on every single sentient being that exists on this planet and in all worlds.

So how can we not respect the very objects that are pushing us toward Enlightenment? You may think, "How ridiculous!" Let's have an easier example. If there are 500 people and I love 499, how can one person stop me from gaining Enlightenment? Because the very fact that you don't like one shows you that you do not have the quality of Enlightenment. Because if you are enlightened, the enlightened state has no hatred or malice, no arrogance, pride, or hurt.

So if you are uncomfortable with even one, it is not that one that is holding you back; it is your emotion, your subtle defilements not yet purified. In fact, these beings are a precious treasure, because they offer you that great opportunity. When others out of jealousy treat me with abuse, slander, and so on—and that can be applied to all the negative emotions you receive from others—may I cherish them and offer the victory to them.

MEDITATION

What would it be like to have absolutely no need to be right?
To perceive pain and injustice others seem to inflict upon us
as purification of harmful separatist concepts we ourselves
have acted from?

How would my body feel?

How would my emotions feel?

How would my heart and mind feel?

How would I interact with them?

Allow yourself to breathe in these liberating energies and relax within them. Let them become one with you.

VERSE SIX

YOUR ENEMY IS THE PROVIDER
OF ALL YOUR VIRTUE

"Like Jesus we belong to the world,
living not for ourselves
but for others."

Mother Teresa

And if someone I have helped,
One for whom I had great hopes,
Harms me without slightest reason,
May I view him as my holy Guru!

Shantideva tells us that our enemies are the providers of our true virtue. When a person that you have benefited and you have placed great hope in hurts you, it is not that person who has hurt you. It is your wrong intent, wrong motive, and wrong projection toward that person that has hurt you.

You have projected onto that person. You have labeled that person "I have helped them, therefore they have to help me." You have a secret expectation. So it is your projection of how that person should treat you and not fulfilling that projection that has hurt you, but not that person.

If you don't put wrong projections on other people, you will not suffer. If you accept others as they are, for who they are and what they are without succumbing to projections, you will not be disappointed. The disappointments in life regarding other people are the projections we put on others, of how we think they should be, how they should act, how they should practice, how they should talk, how they should eat, how they should react. And when they don't fulfil that expectation, they are bad. We have to get them back. They are not good.

No! You have received that harm because of your own negative karma; you have created the results, because if that person is truly bad, everybody must see that person as bad or that object as bad. Certainly there are some people who love that person and there are some that hate that person, which means that the love and hate is not intrinsically that person, but your projection of that person.

A simple example: if there is a yellow flower, everybody will see it as yellow unless they are color blind. So when you see that flower and you see it as yellow, or when you see the beautiful golden pandit hat of Je Rinpoche as yellow, if that object is inherently yellow itself, then everybody will see it as yellow. But when we see a person and we say they are bad, or they are not good, or they are good, it is not that they are bad or they are good; it is our projection of that person. And our projection and our view of that person may not always be accurate, because we are not filled with compassion; we are not filled with wisdom. We don't have such positive karma to see the true reality of other people or to see their karma.

So when we get disappointed with people or people supposedly hurt us, it is not that person. And if you react, it shows your deep ignorance and very strong wrong and negative conditioning, and your negative reaction to your own negative projection. So even if that person is negative—let's presuppose and hypothetically say that that person is negative, and they have wronged us—it still does not give us the permission to wrong them. So either way, we are wrong. Either way, we collect negative karma. But basically, most sufferings come about from our wrong projection, our expectation of how a situation should be.

We think, "Oh! I have a girlfriend, she's wonderful, she's beautiful, she's fabulous, she's loyal, she's honest, she's hard-working, she's smart, she's clean, she's neat, she's efficient. She's beautiful and she's fabulous, that's why I love her." You get married—she's a slob, she never cleans up, she takes a bath once a week, she has a bad temper. She won't wash your socks—you have to do it yourself. And right after you got married, she gained 30 pounds—surprise! You are disappointed. You are disillusioned. You suddenly find you don't love her anymore.

The reason why marriages have difficulties and sometimes unfortunately fall apart, or relationships between men and women do not work out in a worldly term, is because of all the projections we have put on that person and that relationship, and it did not fulfill our projections. Our wife should be like that, she should be like this, she should act like that, she should act like this. He should be like that—blah, blah, blah, blah.

Okay, she's *not* like this, she's *not* like that, so cut it out. Accept her as she *is*. It's the very projection you put on that person and when they don't fulfill the projection, you suffer, you cry, you become depressed. Who is at fault?

Unfortunately, we work and act out of our projections. We feel that a person should be nice to us, and if they are not, we abuse them, we fight back, we round up people against them. We have a hate campaign against that person, yet we never win. It shows clearly our negative state of mind, our lack of understanding, our lack of compassion, our lack of patience and practice, and our lack of realization of the kindness of enemies, of people that abuse us.

So in fact, you should see that person as a great teacher. What type of teacher? Someone who teaches you what you should not act like. They are giving you a chance to see your state of mind in that condition, in that situation. So we need to stop projecting what we feel and what we want, what we think that person should be, and instead accept that person for what they are, who they are, and how they are. If we can accept that and be *with* them, a lot of our problems are solved. If we cannot, and we expect this and wish this and want that and that and that, we suffer. We are suffering and we will continue to suffer.

No one is perfect; no one is wonderful. The conditions for someone to be perfect are impermanent. The conditions for someone to be imperfect are impermanent too. Don't be attached to either. Don't be attached to someone who is not nice, and harp on it and think about it and think about the abuse that they have given you, because it is impermanent. They can change; you can change. Hopefully you change before they do. People who are wonderful could become not wonderful. So don't be attached to them; be detached, knowing that it is impermanent and both situations will stop, will end.

Your projections on those situations will create suffering and your reaction in regards to your projections will increase it even more.

Let's start accepting people for what they are and how they are; let's have compassion. If they need help, help them. And sometimes we can help them by just not reacting and not fighting back. Sometimes we can help them more by not fighting or reacting, and just letting it go—even if we have to do it a hundred times—because it helps us. Because if we can do it a hundred times, it shows you we are advancing, we are getting better.

MEDITATION

What would it be like to perceive the deepest hurt as the highest teacher? To realize that while there is a place in me that can be hurt I am not free of personal motives and to be grateful to those who in this way invite me to rediscover unconditional freedom and love?

How would my body feel?

How would my emotions feel?

How would my heart and mind feel?

How would I interact with them?

Allow yourself to breathe in these liberating energies and relax within them. Let them become one with you.

VERSE SEVEN

GIVING AND TAKING

May Love and Compassion
be your teacher,
the best of friends,
your true companion.

HH Dalai Lama

In brief, directly and indirectly,
I offer aid and joy to all my mothers!
May I secretly take upon myself
All harm and suffering of my mothers!

What is that saying? When your beautiful, wonderful, kind and very compassionate mother conceived you—and in general terms, it is out of great love—from the moment she found out that you were in her body, she loved you. The very thought of you being in her body created happiness. From the minute you kicked, the minute you created discomfort for her, although she was uncomfortable, she was happy. She protected you when you were in the womb. She bore the burden of a heavy being in her body for months upon months. She cared for you by not taking extremely cold foods or hot foods. She cared for you by sitting down gently and rising gently, so that you, as a little, unborn child in her body, would not feel physical discomfort.

When it was time for you to be born and before that, how much suffering you created for your mother in the sense of nausea, morning sickness, pains, discomfort! And then when you finally issued forth from your beautiful, kind, wonderful mother, how much pain did you cause her? How much stretching of her body did you cause? How much blood did she lose, how much sweat, how much screaming, how many hours of intense pain? And even with that pain, she was still happy. Some children even cause death to their mothers. And yet when the mother is dying, she wants to make sure that her child is alright and well, even with the last dying breath. And the minute the child, that being that has caused so much pain and discomfort for months upon months upon months upon months is issued forth, instead of slapping and kicking and beating and abusing that little, evil thing that causes so much trouble and pain, she grabs the child and hugs that child in her fatigue to her breast and loves the child. How kind is the mother!

And then your mother, from the moment you issued forth, voluntarily surrenders her freedom. She has no freedom to sleep, no freedom to eat, no freedom to beautify herself or to go out. She is at the mercy of every whim, noise, and fuss of that little child. That little child has become the center of her world and all her energies are focused on that child.

From being awake at night for the child, she gets lines under her eyes. She loses her figure. She suffers incredible pain and she can even become unhealthy because of that child. She completely loses her freedom. She will work, fight, and sacrifice her time, energy, and effort for that child. She will even give up her life for that child if necessary, without a blink of an eye. And when that child is sick, she is worried to no end; when the child is happy, she is happier than the child itself. When the child grows up, when the child is successful, when the child is doing well, the mother sincerely, wholeheartedly rejoices for the child. And when the child falls down or when the child is not successful, the mother suffers because of love and deep compassion for that child.

How kind is that mother! The very flesh on us that we use to do Dharma practice, the very flesh that we have comes from our mother. The very bones and flesh that we have come from our mother. In that respect, women are much greater than men. Incredible! Their bodies are more frail, smaller, more delicate, yet they can produce a greater result. And in Tantra, we should respect women and see women as the equal of men, if not better. That is why we have Buddhas like Tara and Vajrayogini and Palden Lhamo. It shows you there is no state of difference between a male and a female.

And the kindness of a mother in normal cases is such that you cannot repay it back. And yet, perhaps, because of lack of time and energy due to all her preoccupations with you, your mother does not have Dharma or is not able to practice the Dharma and is ignorant and suffers; she will have to die and take rebirth, and maybe even take rebirth in hell. This kind mother who has done so much for you might have to take rebirth in hell or one of the lower realms.

Yes, she may have done things that hurt you. Maybe she has said things that hurt you. Maybe she doesn't understand you. Maybe you don't have a wonderful relationship with her, but that doesn't deny the fact that everything you have comes from her.

Whatever we do, we can never repay the kindness of a mother—ever! We can give her 50 million dollars, but we can still not repay the kindness of that mother to us. All the intensity of her love and her patience and her energy toward us, we can never repay it.

So if she says unkind things to us because of her own delusions from previous lives, we should forgive her. We should in fact see it as pleasure and beautiful. We should serve her. We should take care of her. We should watch her in her old age. We should be at her beck and call, and we should treat her as we treat our own Guru. Every moment that we have with our mother is a very precious moment, and we should not let it slip by. And if due to our bad karma our mother passed away, we should never forget her kindness and practice the Dharma for them and dedicate it to them, such a kind being that has been so wonderful to you and suffered so much pain and difficulty for you. Can we be so ungrateful not to repay her kindness and not to treat her like a queen?

Like that, in your previous lives you had a mother, and the life before that you had a mother. And in some situations, with respect to the mothers in this life, some mothers from previous lives maybe even have sacrificed their lives and gave more than your mother of this life. We just cannot remember at this time. So in every single life, thousands upon thousands and millions and millions of lifetimes we had a mother who treated us like the mother of this life.

Therefore, in Mahayana Buddhism, we say "all mother sentient beings" or "all mothers." It doesn't mean that these four monks sitting here are my mothers. It doesn't mean that everybody is my mother. It means that at one time or another, every single sentient being has been your mother and has treated you in such a way and don't you think you should repay that kindness back? Whether it was done in this life or previous life, it was done to *you*. You got that benefit, that's why you are here today. Don't you think you should repay their kindness?

Therefore, in Mahayana Buddhism, the first step to developing Bodhicitta is the recognition that all sentient beings have been your mothers, on that logical basis.

And therefore all mother beings—some of them are in hell, some of them are in the spirit world realms, some of them are animals, some of them are in desperate human situations, some are all around you, some in the god realms— taking rebirth and suffering again and again in samsara, how can you, an ungrateful child, let your mothers suffer? Recognize that is the first step toward achieving Bodhicitta.

In short, may I do whatever I can to directly and indirectly help my mothers. May I offer all the benefit to them and take their sufferings, openly and secretly endure suffering for my mothers who have been so kind to me. May I secretly take upon all mother sentient beings' sufferings and pain.

We should pray for that quality. We should want that quality, yearn for it, make offerings for it, meditate for it. We should recite mantras or do retreats for it. We should go to our Gurus for it, and receive teachings for it. We should make donations and do whatever beautiful charity works that everybody has been doing for that purpose and that purpose alone: to repay the kindness of mother sentient beings. How to repay them? Not simply to give food, clothing, shelter, and medicine, but to give them the complete method to be free from samsara. And the only way you can do that is by becoming an enlightened Being for their sake.

"For the sake of all mother sentient beings I will listen to the Dharma, so that I will learn the methods and I can practice and I can become an enlightened Being to repay their kindness. For the sake of all mother sentient beings, I will make offerings; for the sake of all mother sentient beings, I will support the beautiful Dharma centers; and from the merit that I receive, may I become a Buddha to benefit my mothers. I will practice patience for my mothers. I will meditate and do mantras for my mothers."

When your motivation is that you will do Dharma practice, help Dharma centers, assist others, and so on, so that you can repay the kindness of others, you will not be disappointed easily when you meet harsh people. You will not be disappointed easily if you do not get results quickly. You will not be disappointed easily if something goes wrong; you will be able to endure it. We can endure a lot of pain and problems for our mothers today, remembering their kindness. So what is the difference between our mother of this life and previous lives?

And there's a very strong chance that the beings around you will be your mothers again. Like H_2O molecules—water molecules, evaporation, cumulus clouds, hail, snow, rain, and then collection of a water body and again evaporation—it is the same H_2O molecules in a cycle. There is not one new H_2O molecule in the world. Like that, there is not one new sentient being in this world. They are the same ones that you will be meeting again and again and again. So doesn't it behove us to remember the kindness of the past and of the present, and the kindness that they will display in the future?

So every action we do, the motive should be *for all mother sentient beings*. And when you do that, you are practicing the Dharma and you are on the way to Buddhahood. Every single Buddha acts out of that compassion, out of that thought, spontaneously, effortlessly, constantly, because they have conditioned and trained.

So we should wake up in the morning and think, "How can I benefit mother sentient beings?" Before we go to sleep, we should think, "How have I benefited others?" And every day to put into our heart, "I will do everything for the sake of other sentient beings. I will be able to endure for others." You will see your mental strength grow; you will see your perseverance grow. You will see your enthusiasm grow. You will see yourself become stable and steady, and that's what we want.

So the motive for anything we do in Dharma should not be the eight worldly concerns. (Yes! It's that crazy monk talking about the eight worldly concerns again!) We should work and do actions not for the center, not for our Gurus, not for friends, not for reputation, not for karma, not for ourselves. We should do it for the sake of sentient beings.

I will help the Dharma centers for the sake of all sentient beings. I will listen to the Dharma for the sake of all sentient beings. I will practice Dharma for the sake of all sentient beings. I will meditate, do mantras, do retreats, go to holy places, I will work and then draw pain and I will put up and show patience to people that hurt me and damaged me and situations that bothered me for the sake of all mother sentient beings.

Why? In short, because you wish to become a Buddha to repay their kindness—to give them the ultimate way to come out of suffering. The only way is to develop those qualities and the only way to develop those qualities is to come across the situations that help you develop those qualities.

So are not sentient beings precious? The Buddha said, you should respect sentient beings 50 percent and respect the Buddha 50 percent. The respect you accord to sentient beings and to the Buddha is equal, because without the Buddhas, you cannot become enlightened, and without sentient beings, you cannot become enlightened. So if you have a Buddha teaching you compassion, and you don't have anywhere to practice it, you cannot become enlightened; 50-50, it says clearly. You are 50 percent dependent upon the Buddhas for Enlightenment, for their teachings, for their inspirations, for their blessings, and so on as the merit field, and you are 50 percent dependent on other sentient beings, especially the ones that you revile, that you do not like.

So if for the sake of all mother sentient beings we do our sadhana or any Dharma action, we will not become disappointed easily, we will not become upset easily, we will not give up easily. We will in fact practice harder and harder and more and more, and therefore, in time, we are able to endure more. Mentally, we become stronger and better and more beneficial. That will be the result of this practice.

When you practice Dharma and then experience negative things, it's a very good sign; it means your karma is being purified quickly. You have to purify the karma sooner or later—it's better to purify now and get it over with. If you have to purify later, the karma will increase.

For example, if you have the karma to wear a coat and you wear it in Alaska or where it is very cold, it is very beneficial. If you wear a coat and walk around at 1 p.m. in the afternoon in Malaysia, the karma is still to get a coat—wearing it is the same, the karma is the same, the coat is the same, but environmentally it is different. So if you have a lot of negative karma and you suffer that karma here, because the environment is easier, the sufferings will be less although the karma is the same. Whereas if you keep the karma and you hold it for later, and it manifests in another environment it will be more severe.

If you have the karma to get sick, try to purify it before it happens, to lessen and mitigate the results. If you have the karma to get sick in Malaysia where everything is modern and there are good hospitals and there are 24-hour clinics, it's very easy. Whereas if you get sick somewhere in the Sahara desert, what are you going to do? The karma to get sick is there; the manifestation of the karma is there. You have to get sick; you suffer the same thing, but the place or the conditions or the environment where you have the karma manifest is very important.

Therefore, while you are practicing the Dharma, don't have wrong view that you should not get sick, should not have poverty, and should not suffer, have problems, and mental difficulties. You should not think like that because the very fact that you are practicing Dharma and these things are manifesting is a very good sign. It's better to suffer sickness, ill health, depression, and unhappiness here where you have relatives, friends, and Dharma brothers and sisters to talk to you and you have your Guru to consult.

When you practice the Dharma deeply and well, yet many negative things happen, they were going to happen anyway but it's good they happened early. It is finished, and in fact when you practice the Dharma and negative things happen, 99 percent of the time you can be sure that its effects are much lessened, compared to if it happened with you *not* practicing the Dharma.

If you do a lot of mantras on Je Tsongkhapa and pray to Je Tsongkhapa to purify your karma, maybe you were supposed to have a car accident but did not. When you pray very hard and if you do meditation correctly and you do the prayers well to Je Tsongkhapa, maybe you still have the car accident, but you come out unharmed or slightly scratched. Whereas if you meditate even more and further, maybe you don't have the car accident but you *dream* you have a car accident and in that dream you suffer tremendously, you suffer all the emotions, anguish, pain, fear of death, fear of loss of your loved ones, relatives and separation. You suffer tremendously in the dream.

What's the difference, suffering in real life or in a dream? The suffering is the same, the difference is that the karma is purified without physical effect.

Therefore when you practice the Dharma, when you do pujas, when you do prayers and meditations, when you make offerings, when you serve your Gurus, when you serve the Sangha, it is meant to purify the negative karma and collect positive karma. So when we are doing Dharma practices and sufferings and problems come along, a great practitioner—one who understands the Dharma with wisdom—is happy. When real Dharma practitioners have sickness, they are uncomfortable, tired, exhausted, or maybe they are in pain, thirsty or hungry; yet they are able to endure any type of suffering happily and easily. Although they endure these problems, they do not suffer. That's the difference: *they do not suffer.*

We endure pain with suffering because we are attached to ego. When we are attached to ego, we don't want to have suffering; we are selfish. We don't care if other people have it; *we* don't want it. Whereas if you endure pain without attachment, you can endure it; you don't suffer. In fact, the very pain that you have increases your happiness. How? You are accepting the pain, the problems, and the difficulties for the sake of others.

So if someone was to say, "If you sacrifice your life, a thousand people will be saved," most of us say "Yes, I'm scared, but I can." If we were to suffer for only one person, we'll think about it. Like that, when we suffer for the Dharma, we suffer for others. We can endure hunger, thirst, sickness, unhappiness, criticism, back-biting, people who go against us, people who do not want to co-operate, and financial or physical problems. When we can endure those kind of things for the sake of the Dharma, for the sake of others, the very karma that made us have those sufferings becomes purified in the process. And by being happy about it and accepting it, you do not create further karma for that to happen in the future.

When we do Dharma practices and we have difficulties and problems, we should try to develop the mind that can take the problems, that can feel the problems, take them and accept them. So in fact when we practice the Dharma, we are able to purify the problem simultaneously while we are dealing with it.

The incredible thing about suffering with or without Dharma is that with Dharma, you purify your karma while you are suffering. Whereas without Dharma, while you are suffering the negative results of karma, you create further ones by reacting back negatively.

For example, if someone criticizes you, "Oh, you are not a good Dharma practitioner" or "You don't know how to chant nicely," it hurts, but that pain and hurt has a cause. You have created the cause; you have said that or done that to someone else in the past to receive that back. Maybe it was not the same exact words, but the intent was the same. When you receive it back and understand that it is from your own karma, you accept it with responsibility and you don't fight back. You keep quiet and contemplate. In that way, while you're suffering, you can purify the karma to have received that suffering, and you do not create further karma to get more suffering.

If you don't have Dharma and someone criticizes, don't you fight back? Don't you defend yourself by saying, "No, I'm not like that. My motive is not like that; my thinking is not like that"? People explaining themselves a lot is a sign of very heavy ego, a very strong ego. It's self-grasping, because they want people to know that they are right, that they are correct, that they are good and that they are better than you.

Explain when we are asked—explain gently, with good words and without gossip and back-biting. It's very important, because when someone talks negatively about us and we go around explaining to everybody, our real intent is to let them know that we are right and they are wrong. In that process, we collect even more negative karma to be even more misunderstood. (And the very purpose for us to explain is to be understood. Isn't that just a terrible irony?)

So, in fact, as Dharma practitioners, we should be able to be happy to endure sufferings for others. We should develop a mind that we can suffer for others, bear difficulties to benefit others, bear problems for the benefit of others. If they criticize you, if they say negative things about you, even if they try to threaten you, if they hurt you, if they try to defame you, let them. Don't fight back, don't harm them back, because two wrongs do not make a right.

As a Dharma practitioner who believes in the Three Jewels, one should "accept the unjust loss and offer the victory to others." And in the beginning, when we do that, some people might try to take advantage of us, but in the end everybody will understand our motive and intention, and we will be loved and be liked and protected by others.

There were many people who tried to take advantage even of Lord Buddha—like his evil cousin, Devadatta. Buddha never reacted. So whether we react negatively or not is whether we understand and practice the Dharma or not. We don't need to practice deep, long Dharma. We don't have to make silly excuses that we are new, but knowing this phrase "offer the victory to others and accept the unjust loss" is very powerful, and in that, we develop mental strength, mental capacity, and mental forbearance to be able to take upon ourselves the sufferings of others. When we are able to do that, we are entering the Bodhisattva path, the path of becoming a Bodhisattva, a Buddha.

And it all starts from this moment, this time. We think, "May I accept the unjust loss and offer the victory to others," and the first person we can start with is our Guru, the one who gives us teachings, the one who is compassionate to us, the one who cares about us, the one who gives us the holy method to become a Buddha to be free from suffering. His or her knowledge, his compassion, her wisdom, her knowledge is much greater than your worldly knowledge, your worldly achievements, and your worldly plans—much greater. We should have due respect for their knowledge, compassion, and love. Although we may scorn and say negative things and go against our teachers, our teachers will always be there for us, will always have compassion for us and will always be ready to accept us. Doesn't that show us something?

We should learn to endure pain, suffering, unhappiness, difficulties, problems, and disasters, with the realization of the results from our karma and that we do it for others. We should be able to endure that difficulty for others. We should develop that mind whether we are religious or we are not religious. Whoever you are, that thought will benefit you in your life. That thought is good for you as a human being, so don't think this is a Buddhist thought. This is a thought that is the truth.

TRUTH IS ONE.

Buddhism expresses the truth in one way. Islam or Hinduism may express the truth in another way, but all is the truth. So with respect to all religious traditions that speak the truth, bear suffering for others, bear difficulties for others. Be able to put up with pain for others until you reach the point when you actually meditate and suffer for others. Take the suffering upon you and suffer for them secretly, without them knowing. Then you become a Bodhisattva.

So we must develop that type of mind, we must develop that type of strength, we must develop that type of capacity. Suffer for others, take pain for others, be able to bear the negative comments from others, be able to bear malicious talk from others, be able to bear bad thoughts or bad talking from others. Have compassion for those people who do these things to you. They are victims just like you. I am sure you have done that at one point in our lives, with respect to all of you.

When we did it, we did it out of ignorance. Now that we have the Dharma, we don't do it anymore. Like that, many people don't have the Dharma, or have the bad karma not to practice the Dharma well. Therefore, by the force of their bad karma, they have no choice but to do these kind of negative actions. So how can we add more wood to the fire and burn up the fire more by fighting back? They are already suffering. They are already collecting so much bad karma by doing this, why add to it and have them do more? Why contribute to their suffering? Why contribute to their problems and to their anger? It won't stop your anger, solve your problem, or dissolve your unhappiness, so forgive them.

Forgive them and let go. In surrendering and letting go— forgiving—you gain mental strength. You will be able to deal with even bigger difficulties. That is a Bodhisattva's ideal way of thinking. We should encourage other people toward good thinking, positive thinking.

So when you have difficult people who are overwhelmed by suffering and depression and negative karma, they talk a lot, they create skepticism, they have big mouths, they gossip, they slander, they're rude, treasure them. Don't push them away. Have compassion for them, keep them near you, and help them. Help them in any way you can. Help them emotionally. Help them financially if you can. Help them materially. Help them in any way you can, because if you don't help them, what Dharma are you practicing? Are you more desperate than them?

I am trying to do that in my life. I have some people who disturb me very much, back-biting me. I try my best to show compassion to them, to humble myself and to let them win—I really try that. Sometimes I am successful, sometimes I'm not. because I'm not a Buddha, but I am getting more and more successful. Maybe that comes from maturity, learning, understanding, praying, and collecting more merits or simple surrendering to my Gurus, saying he is correct and I'm not; sometimes it's simple as that.

So I have people too who disturb me, but I don't hate them. I try not to think bad thoughts about them. When they come and see me, I try to be very kind to them and I don't try to be artificial in my plans. I really try to develop this feeling toward them, and then when I've conquered, by compassion, this one person who has harmed me, I can go on to the next one and the next one. And then it becomes easier and easier and easier and easier until I reached the point where they don't disturb me anymore.

"I will take their sufferings upon myself." There are no mantras, there are no miracles, there are no meditations. It's good, old, simple hard work, but it's worth it. If you do it, it's the same situation. If you don't do it, it's the same situation, so it's better to experience the situation, then grow from it and improve from it than just to experience it, react negatively, and then never grow from it. So I think that is very important.

Please hold people who disturb you and create problems and difficulties with compassion. "Near you" doesn't mean you have to keep them on your shoulders and carry them everywhere. "Keep them near you" means in your heart. Help them. Never be tired of helping them. The Buddha is never tired of helping us; our Gurus are never tired of putting up with us. So we should just be as courageous to put up with them and help them materially, financially, food, emotionally, by making them comfortable. Remember Atisha and that monk?

Please don't let these teachings remain here. With all due respect (I don't mean to say you are so bad), please let's not go back to our old selves, our old ways, and our old habits and thinking. Please think about this; let it enter your heart, accept it, and practice it. Not when you are in a good mood, not when you have good business deal, not when you have money in the bank, not when you have harmony, not when you've had your supper, not when you are healthy. Now, immediately! And you'll experience the change.

In this verse, we find the culmination of compassion, where it merges and becomes inseparable from wisdom. Shantideva stated that, without wisdom, there can be no true compassion. Bodhisattvas spontaneously help anyone, because for them there is no "other," no separation, no duality. Every pain of every being is felt as their own, yet welcomed with open arms and without personal suffering. It is the most beautiful and inconceivable mystery, and at the same time nothing could be more natural. It is the never-ending miracle of love, and Bodhisattvas *are* this miracle and nothing else.

MEDITATION

What would it be like to be so free—so everything, so nothing—as to be able to give all my happiness and everything good constantly to everyone, while absorbing all their pain and difficulties with the greatest joy?

To perceive every being as so close to me that to wish them the highest good becomes spontaneous, and their suffering becomes so unbearable to me that I pray for it to come to me instead?

How would my body feel?

How would my emotions feel?

How would my heart and mind feel?

How would I interact with them?

Allow yourself to breathe in these liberating energies and relax within them. Let them become one with you.

VERSE EIGHT

FREEDOM

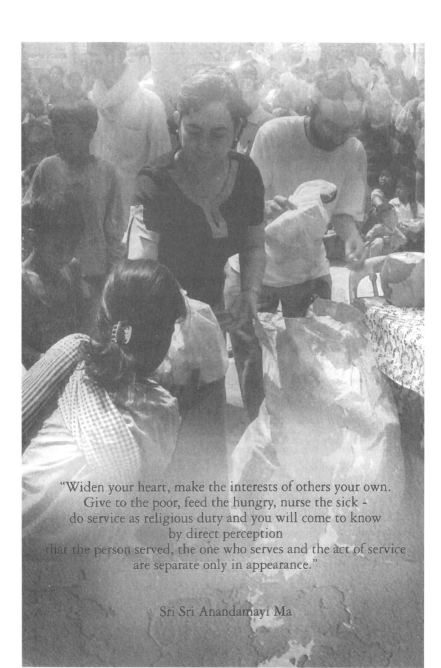

"Widen your heart, make the interests of others your own.
Give to the poor, feed the hungry, nurse the sick -
do service as religious duty and you will come to know
by direct perception
that the person served, the one who serves and the act of service
are separate only in appearance."

Sri Sri Anandamayi Ma

May all of this be undefiled
By stains of the eight mundane views,
And through discernment, knowing all things as illusion,
Without grasping, may all be released from bondage!

The practical secret here is to stop distinguishing between pleasant and unpleasant. By perceiving all phenomena as illusory, by realizing their dreamlike, fleeting nature, we come to see that everything (and nothing) is really the same. Nothing is good or bad in itself. It is the label we attach to it, our projections that seem to make it wonderful or horrible.

Being aware of the ultimately empty, illusory nature of all phenomena empowers us to free ourselves from attachment and aversion. We should apply this view to our entire life, including our spiritual practice. The Masters urge us to be free of subject, object, and act. The one who meditates (subject), the enlightened Being meditated on (object), and the act of meditation are not separate, but a totality. At the same time, each is empty from their own side.

This should become our on-going meditation.

"Empty of inherent existence" doesn't mean that nothing matters and we become indifferent to the pain and needs of others! It is no coincidence that seven of the eight verses help us to relinquish self-grasping and self-cherishing tendencies by cultivating great compassion—relative Bodhicitta—which leads to their complete dismantling through profound insight into the nature of reality, as described in this eighth and last verse which points out wisdom or absolute Bodhicitta. If we practice correctly—free from the extremes of eternalism and nihilism—the opposite of indifference happens: when grasping ceases and wisdom dawns, we become total availability. Non-dual love and compassion reveal themselves as natural expressions of the pristine clarity of this unconditioned awareness. Being finally free of agendas, therefore directly seeing into the heart of each moment, life becomes an ongoing, elegantly flowing creative play and prayer in service of the Great Awakenings of all beings without exception.

Nagarjuna stated that "samsara and nirvana lack even an atom of true existence, while cause and effect and dependent arising are unfailing." To reconcile this apparent paradox, to profoundly realize that "these two are complementary not contradictory," is what is called the Middle Way. Relative and absolute truth, interconnectedness and emptiness, compassion and wisdom are inseparably intertwined, support each other, depend on each other. Truth is One, as Je Tsongkhapa has made visible with brilliant wonderful clarity.

This concludes the eight transformations. These teachings are sacred. These teachings are holy. As coming from an unrealized monk who sincerely believes in these teachings that I have received from the correct source and the correct Guru, I invoke the blessings of His Holiness, Avalokiteshvara, Chenrezig, Tenzin Gyatso, the Dalai Lama, that these teachings may go into your hearts and go straight into the center of your mind, and that you will practice it from this moment onward.

If you practice this and nothing else—and you can check this with His Holiness—you can become enlightened. And you don't need any commitments, except those mentioned in the Eight Verses. If you practice this, all of the 84,000 teachings of Buddha Shakyamuni that He taught for more than 41 years of His holy life, are included in these eight verses.

Please don't chase after mantras, holy places, exotic Gurus with wonderful hats. Don't chase after wonder-Gurus that come from exotic places, that are emanations of deities that you can't even recognize, with so many arms, faces, and colors that they drive you crazy. Don't chase after exotic temples and exotic initiations and empowerments. Don't chase after exotic rituals and pujas because none of that can remove your sufferings and none of that can give you happiness. Only the *Eight Verses of Mind Transformation* and their practice will give you this. Every single practice and meditation, every single method that the Buddha has given you is an extension and elaboration of the *Eight Verses of Mind Training*. So if Mind Training is not practiced in some way, shape, or form you will definitely not gain results.

We can even condense it all into eight small lines:

All beings are infinitely precious.
Practice the humility of a pure view.
Always check the mind.
Be grateful for difficult situations.
Let others win.
True love is unconditional.
Give all joy, take all pain.
Appearances are like a dream; wake up!

This is the complete path of the Buddha right here.

These eight short lines are a condensed form of the Eight Verses and these eight verses are the condensed Bodhicharyavatara (the extended form is the Buddha's complete teachings on compassion).

So the first seven little, simple lines are the complete teachings of Lord Buddha on compassion and the last line is our wisdom. All the teachings are here. I beg you, I implore you, and I ask you, if you really wish to practice the Dharma, read these every day.

I know you have millions of sadhanas and millions of deities and meditational retreats that you have to do. But can I ask you one simple question, with deep respect and no malice intended? Have those exotic deities given you any results? Have those exotic mantras and secret initiations brought you any results? Have you become kinder? If you haven't, we should go back to the basics, because the basics are what *make* those deities. So please stop running after all types of exotic Lamas, me included. Stop running after ego-pleasing Dharma practice. Please follow your Guru's advice and practice the Dharma.

The best pilgrimage is the place you practice the *Eight Thoughts of Transformation*. The best offering you can make to your Guru is to accomplish these eight thoughts and the best temple is where this is taught and practiced. The best center is the place where this is taught and practiced. The best people are the ones that accomplish this.

All Buddhas were born of these teachings. They are being created now from these teachings and will be born from them in the future. Hold these teachings sacred. Frame them, re-type them, decorate them, put flowers around them. Make offerings to these teachings, because they are the Buddha's essence in words. Practice them, memorize them, commit them to heart. Recite them every day and when certain situations come, I guarantee you one of them will pop into your head and you will be able to control yourself. If you practice nothing else, if you don't want anything else at all, this is enough. If you practice this, you will gain Enlightenment.

I am happy to share these wonderful teachings with you that I received from His Holiness. I don't dare say "teach you," but I say *share* these teachings with you. We are all Dharma brothers and sisters. We are all on the same level, and we are all in samsara together so we can share what we have with each other, and that's the most important thing.

> *By realizing that all sentient beings*
> *Are more precious than wish-granting jewels,*
> *For attainment of the supreme goal,*
> *May I always hold them dear to my heart!*

> *Whenever I associate with anyone,*
> *May I view myself as least of all,*
> *And, from the depths of my heart,*
> *May I cherish others as supreme!*

During all actions, as soon as thoughts
Or delusions arise in my mind
That are harmful to myself and others,
May I stop them with effective means!

As for sentient beings who are bad-natured,
When I see they are oppressed by negativity and pain,
May I cherish them just like I am encountering
A precious treasure that is difficult to find!

May I accept unjust loss
Such as others abusing me,
Or slandering me out of jealousy,
And may I offer the victory to others!

And if someone I have helped,
One for whom I had great hopes,
Harms me without slightest reason,
May I view him as my holy Guru!

In brief, directly and indirectly,
I offer aid and joy to all my mothers!
May I secretly take upon myself
All harm and suffering of my mothers!

May all of this be undefiled
By stains of the eight mundane views,
And through discernment, knowing all things as illusion,
Without grasping, may all be released from bondage!

PART THREE

WISDOM

MEDITATION ON IMPERMANENCE

MAY I REMEMBER MY GURU'S INSTRUCTIONS

When the doctor gives up on me,
when rituals and pujas no longer work,
when friends have given up hope for my life,
when anything I do is futile,
may I be blessed to remember
my Guru's instructions.

These words of the Great Panchen Lama sum up the total motive and the total reason to practice the Dharma.

What is he talking about? In the beginning, in the middle, and finally in the end, nothing matters except for our Guru's instructions. And what is our Guru's instruction? Our Guru's instruction is to practice the Dharma. What exactly is practicing the Dharma? To practice the Dharma is transforming our mind from negative states of affliction and emotion to positive states as much as we can.

Death is very near. Death is very soon. Life, time, energy is going by so fast and passing by so fast it's almost unaccountable. But is the time passing by with Dharma or without Dharma? And when I say that, we must look even deeper. When I say with or without Dharma, it means with transformation or without transformation.

If we are stuck on mantras, rituals, prayers, if we are stuck on meditations, teachings, retreats, if we are stuck on visiting holy places yet the mind never ever changes, we have to examine why. We have to check, *why?* We have to check why and we have to check it immediately; we must not delay, and we must not be comfortable that we are not changing and transforming. This is very important.

We should practice the Dharma in order to become a fully enlightened Being, to be of utmost benefit to others and ourselves. You will continuously create positive actions if you are free of the eight worldly concerns and remember death at all times. But if you don't remember death, you will constantly create more negative karma and become more unsuitable for liberation. At the time of death, you will feel intense regret at having wasted your precious opportunity.

Death is certain. No power in the universe can stop your death. Every person that has been born has died. Even the Buddha himself had to die. Within 80 years' time, every single person in this room will be dead. So what will matter at that time that is completely uncertain? Blindly, ignorantly, and delusionally, and out of great conditioning, we make plans, but actually there are no plans to make. Because the plans are not in our hands.

Secret mountains and caves, forests, huge skyscrapers and vaults, and bullet-proof glass cannot protect us from death. There is nowhere to hide.

From the time we are born, from the moment we spring from our kind mothers, we are racing toward death. It's like a bullet train that never stops. There are no stops, there is only a destination. Every breath is getting closer to death. Some people avoid this subject and avoid the truth, thinking that by not facing it, it will not happen.

Imagine, out of the 70 years that we are basically alive, half of it we spend sleeping. The other half is spent working, eating, quarreling, shopping, traveling, and watching television. Very little time is spent on Dharma. And even the very little time that we spend on Dharma, is it really Dharma? That's how rare and precious Dharma is.

When we are young, we put off our Dharma practice until we are stable in life and we have some wealth. When we are middle-aged, we get distracted; every week it's signing another contract and "After that one, I will practice the Dharma." When we get older, we look back and regret the practices that we could have done and did not.

Age is no guarantee. Children or young people often die before older people. Health is no guarantee. Healthy people die before sick people. The very things that are meant to keep us alive can become conditions that actually kill us, such as food, housing, medicine. In general, huge trees, forests, and mountains all can be destroyed, and they are so strong and big and solid. And our bodies are so fragile. Near and dear ones give rise to attachment and pain; no one can share our experience of death.

If you remember death, your Dharma practice becomes pure. Your Dharma actions become powerful and effective, beneficial in the beginning, beneficial in the middle and beneficial at the end, and in the hour of death, you will go with satisfaction, knowing you have spent your life meaningfully. We should be more worried about what's going to happen after death than before death.

"When doctors give up on me, when rituals no longer work, when friends have given up hope on my life, when anything I do is futile, may I be blessed to remember my Guru's instructions"—how incredibly deep.

So when we attend Dharma talks, read this book now, or do any Dharma activities, however minor, we should develop good motivation and constantly propel ourselves to be free of worldly concerns, contemplating on death and impermanence as I have described just now. And afterward, do not go back to your old ways; do not go back to your old habits. Do not think, "That monk is a great actor. He was a great joker; he made us laugh. When is the next show?"

We must contemplate. We must remain silent and not go back to our old ways—not start gossiping, not start talking. We should not start putting other people down, getting angry, fighting. We should practice it immediately. We should take courage and make a difference and practice it immediately—not let it degenerate, but let it excel and grow.

This human form endowed with freedom,
more valuable than a wish-granting gem
obtained only this once,
is difficult to acquire, is easily lost,
passing like a flash of lightning in the sky.
Remembering this and understanding that
all worldly activities are like husks,
at all times, day and night,
you must try to take advantage

of its essential significance.
I, a yogi, have practiced in this way,
you, oh liberation seekers
should do likewise.

Je Tsongkhapa urges us.
May his kindness
be our guide.

This is the essence of the Buddha's teachings.

May we gain Bodhicitta and realization of emptiness—
and by that may we gain full Enlightenment.

And when we gain full Enlightenment
we don't run to Amitabha Heaven,
get on a nice red couch and relax
and sleep and just be free and happy,
but come back again and again
to serve sentient beings until the end of time.

Until the last sentient being
is finished with suffering,
may I continue to take rebirth again
and again and again to benefit others.

Please pray like that and the power will come.

APPENDIX

EXCHANGING "SELF" AND "OTHER"

TONGLEN: GIVING AND TAKING

"Giving and taking," (*Tonglen* in Tibetan), is a supremely powerful method to generate deep closeness with oneself and others while at the same time attacking the roots of the self-grasping and self-cherishing mind. For a long time Tonglen has only been taught to the most advanced practitioners. During Geshe Chekawa's time, it became known as the "Dharma of lepers," because many lepers found their illness cured through this practice.

We calm our body and mind, and take refuge in the enlightened Ones. We remember our truest wish: the unchanging happiness of every living being. Then we start breathing in others' pain and difficulties through the right nostril, visualized as black smoke that enters our heart, completely shattering our self-cherishing mind. The black smoke dissolves simultaneously with our ego. Now, through our left nostril, we breathe out the pure white light of the holiest love and wisdom we can conceive of, seeing and feeling how it fills and heals and transforms all beings until they are in a state of lasting happiness and free of any type of suffering, appearing as female and male Buddhas.

It is recommended to start by visualizing and practicing with someone close to us (this can be ourselves; for most of us this is very important), whose pain we can hardly bear to see. Later we move on to someone neutral and finally to someone we dislike or hate. We gradually expand our practice to include all living beings.

We can elaborate the visualization or simplify it—whatever works to open ourselves to a direct, intimate and transforming experience. His Holiness the Dalai Lama has stated that we can also simplify breathe in others' pain and send them happiness without any visualization. In this way, we can practice anywhere and anytime.

As beginners, we give and take indirectly, through visualization, but with sincere motivation and deep faith nothing is impossible, and one day we can be like the great Masters who radiate blessings and absorb sufferings and karma directly, by simply being present. Because they have gone far beyond any concern for themselves, they are constantly and spontaneously filled with blissful compassion and the fervent longing to serve all beings in realizing their Buddha-nature.

GLOSSARY

Bodhicharyavatara: Considered by many realized Masters as one of the most enlightening texts of all time, an ideal companion for the book you are just reading. Sanskrit for "the way of the Bodhisattva," containing Shantideva's teachings.

Bodhicitta: The altruistic determination to attain Enlightenment in order to free all beings from suffering. In India and Tibet, there were two methods mainly practiced to attain it. One focuses on developing loving kindness towards all (recognizing all beings as having been our mothers, remembering their kindness and determining to bringing them great benefit), the other on exchanging oneself with others. Je Tsongkhapa, in his spiritual genius, combined the two. Just like the other holy faultless Tibetan traditions of Nyingma, Sakya, and Kagyu have their very special extraordinary methods, this particularly powerful way of developing Bodhicitta is one of the wonders of the Gelugpa school of Buddhism.

Bodhisattva: Who dedicates every breath to attaining Buddhahood as directly as possible, so as to liberate every living being as well.

Bomoh: Sorcerer.

Dhana: Offerings to spiritual teachers and communities.

Dharma: The actual object of refuge; enlightening teachings that inspire the correct conduct to realize them.

Great Awakening: Enlightenment.

Guru, Lama: Our spiritual teacher that guides us, life after life if necessary, all the way to Enlightenment.

Guru Devotion: The most direct way to the final surrendering of our dualistic self-grasping mind, which is the source of all confusion and unhappiness, and therefore the quickest way to Enlightenment.

Je Rinpoche: Mahasiddha Je Tsongkhapa, embodying Avlokiteshvara, Manjushri and Vajrapani, the Buddhas of compassion, wisdom and power. Founder of the Gelugpa school of Tibetan Buddhism.

Kowtow: Bow, pay respect, and also prostration.

Lamrim: Je Tsonghapa's miraculous feat of clearly showing the entire path to Enlightenment. One of the most important texts one could ever study.

Lojong: Mind training. Traditional term for the practices described in this book.

Lower Realms: Consisting of three realms: the animal realm—beings who live in fear of being eaten by another, cannot speak, and cannot activate their Buddha nature; the hungry ghost realm—beings who suffer from extreme hunger and thirst; the hell realms—beings who suffer from extreme hot or cold. Strong grasping, greed, and hatred propel us there unless we cultivate selflessness and realize our Buddha-nature.

Mahayana: The great vehicle. Practicing Dharma with the vast aim of benefiting all beings.

Mandala: Symbolic representation of the universe visualized as Buddha Land. Offered to one's spiritual Master or a Buddha as the best we have to give.

Mantras: Prayers that are the spiritual energy of the Buddhas in the form of sound. Reciting mantras evokes the energy of the Buddhas.

Meditational Deity Practice: Connecting via visualization, prayers, and mantras with a Buddha one has a special affinity to. "Downloading" their holy qualities into our system to activate our corresponding holy potential.

Merits: Positive spiritual energy that is needed to activate our enlightened potential.

Metta: Benevolence, friendliness, amity, friendship, good will, kindness.

Nagarjuna: Propounder of the supremely sublime Middle Way philosophy.

Om Mani Padme Hum (pronounced om mani peme hung): Mantra, the spiritual energy of the Buddha of enlightened compassion, Avalokiteshvara (Sanskrit), Chenrezig (Tibetan), Kuan Yin (Chinese), in the form of sound.

Palden Lhamo: One of the main Protectors of Tibetan Buddhism and the main Protector of Tibet. She is the personal Protector of the Dalai Lamas and the Panchen Lamas, and is especially venerated by the Gelugpa practitioners.

Pandita: Sanskrit for scholar. Someone highly accomplished in dharmic studies.

Paramitas: The Six Perfections, also known as the six paramitas. These are the qualities we should aspire to: 1. Generosity 2. Ethical discipline 3. Patience 4. Enthusiastic effort 5. Concentration 6. Wisdom.

Profound Insight: Wisdom; seeing phenomena's actual mode of existence.

Prostrations: They purify negative physical karma and advocate humility. A very profound and important Buddhist practice.

Puja: Liturgy: A set of prayers and mantras performed to clear obstacles and invoke the blessings of enlightened Beings.

Sadhana: A collection of prayers and mantras which are recited on a regular, daily basis, and which help transform our lives by cutting away negative states of mind and developing enlightened qualities.

Samsara: The six realms of conditioned cyclic existence consisting of the three lower realms (hell, spirits, and animals) and the three higher realms (humans, demi-gods, and gods). Each realm has its more or less intense degree of suffering; the human realm is considered most suitable for spiritual practice. Mahayana Buddhists strive to achieve the ultimate goal of Enlightenment in order to liberate all sentient beings from samsaric existence.

Shantideva: Sanskrit for "god of peace," an enlightened Master from Nalanda Monastery in ancient India.

Tantra: Swift, profound practices by which Enlightenment can be attained within one short lifetime.

Tara: The swift saviouress; female Buddha of fearless enlightened activity.

Vajrasattva: Buddha of original purity.

Vajrayogini: The union of bliss and emptiness in ecstatic wrathful female form. Her practice contains the essence of all Tantras and is supremely powerful in our times.

Yidam: Meditational deity to whom one has a special affinity.

HIS EMINENCE TSEM RINPOCHE

Beloved for his unconventional, contemporary approach to Dharma, H.E. Tsem Rinpoche brings more than 2,500 years of Buddhist wisdom and teachings to the modern spiritual seeker by connecting ancient worlds with new people, cultures, attitudes, and lifestyles.

A Mongolian-Tibetan heritage, a childhood in Taiwan and in the United States of America, intensive monastic studies in India, and now the Spiritual Guide of the Kechara organization in Malaysia—these are but some of the many facets that contribute to Tsem Rinpoche's unique ability to effortlessly bridge the East and the West. His teachings bring the Dharma to our everyday lives, and in doing so, he is able to bring the ancient, time-honored Buddhist philosophies and practices into the 21st century.

Tsem Rinpoche has been strongly inclined towards Dharma since his early childhood, and has studied under many great Buddhist masters of the Tibetan tradition. Tsem Rinpoche eventually went on to receive his monastic education at Gaden Shartse Monastery, currently located in Mundgod in South India.

Following the advice of his beloved Guru, H.H. Kyabje Zong Rinpoche, Tsem Rinpoche took his vows as a monk from H.H. the Dalai Lama and joined Gaden Shartse Monastery when he was in his early 20s. His two preceding incarnations, Gedun Nyedrak and Kentrul Thubten Lamsang Rinpoche, had also studied at the original Gaden Shartse Monastery when it was then located in Tibet. There, they obtained Geshe Lharam degrees before completing their studies at Gyuto tantric college.

Gedun Nyedrak went on to become the lead chanter and, later, abbot of Gaden Monastery, while Kentrul Rinpoche brought the Dharma to the laypeople of the Phari district of Tibet. The tremendous and virtuous work of his previous lifetimes can perhaps be reflected again in Tsem Rinpoche's present-day activities in Malaysia, where he continues this selfless practice of teaching vast numbers of non-monastic communities in places where the Dharma has just begun to bloom.

During his nine years in Gaden, Tsem Rinpoche was involved in extensive charitable works, including building schools for refugee children in India, building dormitories and upgrading living conditions for the monastic community, and providing long-term assistance to the poor lay community of Mundgod.

Now, based in Malaysia, Tsem Rinpoche continues this immense work to benefit many. Through creative and engaging approaches, Tsem Rinpoche continuously shares new methods of bringing happiness and relief to people from all walks of life, regardless of their religious faith. Tsem Rinpoche also maintains close contact with Gaden Monastery; through his constant practice of generosity and with a deeply altruistic motivation, he continues to frequently sponsor Gaden's work and activities.

Be inspired by H.E. Tsem Rinpoche's work and life at *www.tsemtulku.com* and share in his personal views, thoughts, and news on his blog at Tsemrinpoche.com.

An Exerpt From

Peace
By Tsem Rinpoche

1 peace begins...

...With the People You Live With

The real practice right now, for all of us, is to bring incredible harmony to every single person who comes into contact with us.

I want you to be fanatical about yourself: your mind, your relationship with the people you love and with everyone around you. That is what Dharma[1] is about.

Dharma is the love, harmony and the greater understanding that a wife and a husband feel for each other. It is when there are fewer arguments between a wife and a husband, between cousins, between siblings, between children and their parents. It brings people closer together.

Temporarily, Dharma may look like it separates families or takes you away from the people you love but I promise you that in the end Dharma will bring everyone closer together. Nothing in the Buddha's teachings talks about breaking people up. Dharma always encourages us to love other people, to forgive our enemies, to live harmoniously with our partners and to create more peace. It has never, ever taught anything else.

Please do not think that Buddha does not want people to have families and be together with the people we love. Buddha is not trying to turn everyone into monks and nuns! That may have been the predominant method and practice during Buddha's time, about 2,500 years ago, but the situation and times have now changed. Buddha set forth different teachings for different time periods which would better suit the people at that particular moment. The 21st Century is not a time for monasticism and holding vows. To be a monk or a nun, for those who can and want to do so now, is certainly incredible and beautiful, but the main Buddhist teachings at this time are about creating inner and outer peace, because peace is very important to all of us, within and without. Right now, we may not be able to do anything about things happening on the outside, but we can do something about what is within, here and around us.

Today, Dharma is about creating beautiful, harmonious relationships with the people around us, to forgive the wrongs that others have done to us and to forgive ourselves also for the wrongs we have done. Then we move on to becoming happy, light, carefree individuals who can bring this light to other people. We must realise that everything that we have is only for a very, very short time. And the most important thing in our lives are the people who care about us—these are the people who have loyally stayed with us and have been by our side through all our bad habits, bad temper, bad words and anger. It is these people—who have stayed with us over time—who are important. In the end, we might lose everything except these people.

We may have had a lot of bad experiences with some of these people but it does not have to remain this way forever—we can change it. And this change begins with very small steps in whatever you are already doing. It is not something monumental and unachievable! If you have one less argument with your partner, that is Dharma. If you have one less attachment, that is Dharma. If you control your anger once a day, that is Dharma. If you forgive your partner, that is Dharma. That is what Dharma is: it is about bringing people together.

Dharma is about harmony, love, care and forgiveness. The most important thing we must learn to do is to let go. Each one of us has very, very strong attachments that have created some form of disharmony within our families, with our husbands, wives, children, friends or business partners.

The disharmony can arise from only a few things, just as illnesses and diseases arise as a result of only a few causes. Generally, if we know the cause of the illness, we can begin to treat it. In the same way, there are only a few things which can cause disharmony within our families or with the people we love: dishonesty, anger towards our partners and not letting them win an argument, greed or miserliness. It could be because we constantly take advantage of our partners, or make them pay and take care of us, and we don't even know it.

We need to really look back at our lives and ask ourselves what is left for us: just death and perhaps a few people around us who will support us, love us and take care of us. What we need to do now is to start doing what we found difficult to do with our partners and friends before.

For example, if you have been having arguments with your wife, you should stop thinking, "Why is my wife like that?" and start to think instead, "Why do I react to my wife like that?" and let go and change yourself. After all, your wife is not going to be a Buddha overnight.

For now, it would be unhelpful for us to talk about world peace, karma,[2] Enlightenment, future lives, etc. Instead, we should just talk about right now, and how much harmony we can bring into our lives and our families. If we are going to pray for and benefit the world, we should begin with the people we live with. We should treasure the people who we are with—I have given you the example of a wife or husband but you can apply that same teaching to children; children should apply that teaching to their parents and siblings.

Stop sitting there bellyaching and complaining about what you do not have. You may never have it for the rest of your life, so do you want to spend the rest of your life complaining about not having it? Or learn to accept it and make others around you happy? We should stop complaining about our partners, friends, children and life. We should stop sitting there, waiting to cash in on a huge fortune and then move on with life. We might never get what we want for the rest of our lives but we need to keep what we already have now.

Stop looking for money, stop looking for the windfall, stop looking for the other person to change, stop looking for outer transformation—look inside and transform immediately. Change yourself, not them. By accepting who they are, it is transformation. Sometimes we may be surprised by what we get back—when we change, they also change, without us even expecting it.

Gifts do not necessarily have to be material. Sometimes, living peacefully with our partners, friends and family, and not screaming and fighting is a gift in itself. If we can pass one day and one week without fighting and shouting, and without disharmony, that is a big gift. We must not wait for the other person to start. *We* have to start. And please do not think that it ends once you have bought a bouquet of flowers for your spouse and done your part. Your effort to bring harmony to your family has to be continuous.

You know what you are inside. You know your good points—which are many—and you know your few flaws. Start Dharma practice today by transforming your few flaws. It is to stop being cold, calculative and angry, and to stop holding on to the past. It is to begin to forgive, to let go of envy and expectations, and to stop blaming and pointing fingers at others.

I am not asking you to chant more, or recite more prayers and mantras[3]; I am asking you to practise real life Dharma. The real practice right now, for all of us, is to bring incredible harmony and love into our families and to every single person who comes into contact with us. Start there.

Our ability and motivation to create harmony does not come from some mystical sign, like Buddha appearing to us in a dream. The motivation comes from knowing that life is very short and we have already made a lot of mistakes. It comes from an awareness of our own shortcomings and knowing that if we let them continue, they will only become stronger and bigger. However, when we face and overcome those shortcomings, and when we are nice to people regardless of whether they are nice to us—that is Dharma.

2 peace begins...

...Even Though Everyone Around You Is a Nightmare

> Spiritual practice is about being nice and patient to people who are not nice to you.

I am sure many of you have nightmare husbands or wives, nightmare children, nightmare partners and friends—in fact, everyone around you is a nightmare! I am sure many of you would like to go into a retreat for a while, where you can be alone, far away from everyone else; or send your nightmare friends and partners into retreat!

Let's fantasise for a moment. Start by thinking about someone who really bothers you. Let's say we advise them to go for a retreat[1] for three years, three months and three days[2] and make up a story about how they will become enlightened by this retreat. If they do not believe in Buddha or Enlightenment, we could tell them that the retreat is for luck and that they will attract a great deal of wealth into their lives by this retreat.

All of us then go up to the Himalayas, find an uninhabited mountain and dig out a cave. We fix it up nicely for their "retreat"—make a little built-in toilet, fix up the cave with curtains and heating, install a water supply, pull wiring from Kathmandu up to the Himalayas, install a generator and make sure they stay up there nice and warm. We even put in a CCTV connection there so they can see what we are doing back at home. Then, we lock them in from the outside as they do in Tibetan-style retreats. We are the only ones who have the key and there are no locksmiths in the Himalayas!

Visualise: The helicopter pad is upstairs, and we are all getting in. We are now all inside the helicopter with that one person we would like to send for retreat and we are about to take off. It is a 16-hour ride to the Himalayan mountains but we are happy to do it—for Dharma, we will put up with anything.

We land on top of Mount Everest and we climb out of the helicopter. We open the little door and show them their new apartment in the Himalayas. We are so excited we almost faint! We put them inside the apartment and now, we are turning the key to lock them in. We run back to the helicopter, we climb in and we fly back to Kuala Lumpur.

And now, they are gone.

Those monster partners and friends are in retreat. We do not have to hear their voices again, we do not have to listen to them rant and complain, we do not have to put up with their hang-ups, their weird quirks, their likes and dislikes, and their attachments. We come back home, all by ourselves—no more nagging, no more arguments, no more weird conversations or ideas. Nothing. Wouldn't that be great?

Think about it. What would be easier? Creating this whole scenario or transforming ourselves and learning to look differently at the situation around us? The things that bother us about that person *are real*. But wouldn't it be easier if we just changed ourselves? There are things that bother us about that person, but there will be something else, or something similar, that will bother us about another person. There are only a few things that we can be disturbed by. It would be one thing or another, a combination or a different manifestation of the same thing. It would therefore be easier to transform ourselves first.

When we are trying to engage in spiritual practice, we should actively look for difficult people—they are the best way for us to learn how to transform our minds from negative ways of thinking to open, positive ways of thinking that can embrace difficulties and benefit the other person.

Personally, I want to meet all the people who do not like established religions. I like the people who say they don't want to meditate, who are lazy and greedy. I want to meet the druggies, the prostitutes, the people who are transgendered and the people who have alternative lifestyles. I want to meet all the people who society labels as strange, weird and different. There is a bigger group of those people out there. I do not want to just meet and talk to the holier-than-thou, saintly, good-as-gold people.

The people who I would like to reach out to are people who are just like you and me, who would not normally engage in spiritual practice, who are not interested, who are lazy, who have a lot of weird ideas, who would rather hang out doing nothing or who are preoccupied with other things—those are the people who make up the majority of the planet. Even when we look at people who are already within established religions, how many of them are really practising what their religions teach? The ones who really practise make up only a very small group.

Many religions cater to these "good" people because it is "easy." It is easy to be nice to someone who is nice to you. They are nice to you, so you are also nice to them. That is not religion; that is not spirituality; that is not Catholicism; that is not Jesus; that is not Buddha; that is not God. It is easy to be nice to someone who is nice to you, but it is not easy to be nice to someone who is *not* nice to you. Religion and spiritual practice is about being nice and patient to people who are *not nice to you*. This is how we bring spirituality to others.

3 peace begins...

...Inside "Boobali" and Respecting Female Energy

All women are *dakinis* and they hold up half the sky.

All women are *dakinis*[1] and we should accord them the respect as such. In Buddhism, women are considered the pillars of the family. They provide emotional strength, they are gentle and feminine, yet strong; they are miracle workers. Their energy is wisdom. They produce children and they give their male companions what they want. They give us company and they support us. In Asian societies especially, women are incredible because they are taught to put up with a lot of things from men and they do put up with these things. Women are treasures and we have to respect them as treasures.

Traditionally, what men want is not to come home to a nagging wife who rants and raves, and complains about everything. Men feel that they have worked all day and they just want to come home and have their wives make a nice home for them. Men want their women to be nice little wives, to stay home, to always give them respect and not to cause them any embarrassment. Men like to sit there, be served and be given things. It does not matter if it is wrong or right. In every old culture, tradition has dictated that women serve men.

It is up to you if you wish to follow tradition or if you want to follow logic; that is not really my business. I am not here to change 20,000 years of society and culture. But what I am trying to say is that however we are served by others, we will have to serve others one day. The karma will come back. Everyone wants something from each other. That's natural, isn't it? So why don't we give that to each other? It is something very small.

So take care of your wives—they are *dakinis*, they gave you your children, they give you a lot of pleasure, they gave you company, they have stayed through thick and thin with you. Give back. Imagine yourself running around for nine months with a huge belly! Buddha recognized the value of female energy and made the female Buddhas Vajrayogini[2] and Tara[3] most supreme in the hierarchy of the practices. It is not because women are better than men but—as even Mao Tse Tung recognized—women hold up half the sky.

We need to stop sitting there expecting women to do things for us, we need to reward them. Tomorrow or the day after, immediately, go and buy some flowers for your wife. Yes, it is a little embarrassing and you feel a little stupid but it does not matter. The stupidity and the embarrassment are over really quickly. You have money for your drinks and friends but you do not have money for your wives? That isn't good.

Don't be embarrassed. I know that for some of you, after being married for twenty years, you've never even given one *petal* to your wife. So now that you give her flowers, she might wonder what your motive is! It's definitely not *boobali*!⁴ Some of you haven't had *boobali* with your wives in over fifteen years! I asked some of you when was the last time you had *boobali*, and you couldn't remember!

But it's not really about *boobali*; it's about inside *boobali*. It is the feeling you get from *boobali*—the warmth, the forgiveness and the care—because time is short. So take care of your wives, bring them flowers once every two or three months. Take them out, with no motive. Don't just take them out to the market or to a cheap café and say, "I took you out, so keep quiet now!" Isn't your wife worth a few hundred dollars for a night out?

What are you saving your money for? What are you keeping it for? Even Tutankhamun couldn't take any of the pyramids and all the wealth inside them with him. It's in the British museum now. What do you think you're going to take with you to your next life when you die? Your 100,000 or 200,000 dollars? Remember, you came into this life naked, just holding on to the placenta.

And women, what can you do for men? You know what they want. Men only want one thing. *Just one thing*—to stop being nagged! So just shut up! Don't nag them. You know how men are not expressive, they don't like to talk about things, they don't want to tell you things. So stop nagging your husbands, ranting, complaining and making noise.

I am not just talking about doing that to husbands; I am also talking about your friends, your mother, your aunt or whoever you nag the life out of. Stop. What's the big deal? It's a small price to pay, a very small gift to give back. You get flowers, they don't get nagging—then you get a little bit closer.

And children must serve their parents. You must do this if you want to practice Buddhism, go into retreat, do your *sadhanas*[5] and accomplish things that are of value. Take a look at the children who serve their parents and those who don't serve their parents, and see where they are in life, where their mental level is and how good their minds are.

Even if they cannot serve their parents physically, children who serve their parents mentally—by not fighting back or helping in whatever way they can—usually have a mental attitude that is more pliable, nicer and kinder. They have achieved more in life. The kids who don't get anywhere in life are the ones who don't serve their parents. There's nothing magical here—they show you the nature of their mind and how deep their selfish mind is.

No one in your life, directly or indirectly, has been kinder to you on a physical level than your parents. No one. (This could also be an aunt or uncle who has taken care of you or anyone who has been kind to you—it does not have to be your biological parents.) If you don't take care of and serve your parents, why do you have them? You're doing your *sadhanas* and prayer retreats, and making offerings but you are not holy in any way and you will not gain any attainments if you do not serve your parents. To serve one's parents is a measuring stick of how intense our selfish mind is or not, and of our attainments.

So if you can, serve your parents intensely. If they don't need you physically or if they don't need your service, then serve them mentally. If they don't need your service mentally, then at least don't be a burden to them in any way, now or in the future. That is service to your parents. If we are a burden for them in the past, the present and the future, we are extremely selfish people and we will not get anywhere in our Dharma practice. We will never get anywhere even in life because how we treat our parents reflects our attitude.

Stop looking at your parents' few flaws or thinking that your expectations were not fulfilled. That is a result of your own karma. Holding on to that, and saying that you are not nice to your parents because they didn't do this or that for you is actually a cover-up for your own very selfish mind.

Serve your parents, drive them around, eat with them, call them, take care of them, listen when they talk to you, listen to them with a smile when they tell you the same story 5,000 times and happily ask them what happened, again and again and again. Give them massages and make time for them. Do you know why? Because that's all that's left.

If you don't serve your parents in a physical, mental way, you are not a Dharma practitioner. If you do any higher practices, such as Vajrayogini or Heruka,[6] you will gain zero attainments and zero progress. In fact, you will go backwards. You might do the practice for years but nothing will happen.

If you are asking why you are still the same, it is because you do not serve your parents and because the measuring stick of the selfishness of the mind has not lessened. And if your selfishness has not lessened, how can you progress in your *sadhanas*? That is why we do the preliminary practices, which transform the mind to make it pliable and ready for tantric practice. Don't think you just do tantric practice and your life changes.

If you want to do Tantra, you need to take care of your parents, the people who have been kind to you and the people around you—your wives and your husbands. You need to be kind. Don't expect people to serve you; *you* serve them and help them. Don't wait for people to give you things; *you* do it.

Every time someone gives you a cup of tea, and you expect it, you collect the karma and you re-habituate the selfish mind. You harm yourself. You get the moment's thrill but ultimately, it is not good. Don't sit there and wait for money from someone. If you really need it and you get it, it's wonderful; but don't blackmail and manipulate for it.

The message here is that it's time to bring Dharma home. I want everyone to make an effort. If you think of me as your Lama,[7] spiritual guide or teacher, that is my instruction to you. If you think of me as a friend, that is my request. If you think of me as a nice person who has lived life and who knows a little bit more, this is me on my knees begging and pleading with you. It doesn't matter to me how you wish to view me. But you need to do that. You need to lessen the mind that brings harm to yourself.

I'm talking about family values, and welding families and people together, because peace and love come from that. Even when we do ceremonies for monks and nuns here in the future, it is not about taking people away from their families; it is about letting them live in austerity for a while to realize how much they have.

I want your *sadhanas* not to be another mantra or another initiation, running after another Lama. How many living Buddhas have you been sitting in front of and getting initiations from? And look at you, you're worse! You're not a living Buddha, you're a living nightmare! You don't need any more initiations and practices and all that. What you need is to take your mother and father out for dinner once a week, to take your wife or husband out for dinner once a week, to not nag your husband. Listen when people tell you what is wrong with you and then stop being that way.

You want to do a *sadhana* every week? That is it. Do something for the very people that you live with, immediately, because that is Dharma, that is your *sadhana*. I'm not telling you to go home and chant mantras. Do you want to be spiritual? Buy flowers for your wife and take her out for a meal. Stop nagging your husband. Don't cheat on your husbands and wives, in any way. You want the greatest *Yidam*?[8] The greatest *Yidam* is getting behind a steering wheel and taking your mother or father out to eat. You want the greatest mantra? The greatest mantra is, "How are you Mummy? How are you Daddy? What can I do for you?" That is the greatest mantra, at this moment, for us.

Do you know what's the greatest mind? The greatest mind is not wanting other people to change, but you yourself changing and accepting other people. The greatest mind is to stop wondering when they will change. No. You should think instead, "When will *I* change?" That is the greatest practice.

So, if you believe in God, that's fabulous; if you believe in Buddha, that's fabulous; if you don't believe in anything, that's fabulous. But please believe in yourself and please believe in the happiness you can bring to people around you. Believe in that. Wouldn't that be lovely?

Continue reading in
Peace by Tsem Rinpoche
978-1601633538